THE VIA MEDIA

By the Same Author

EVERYMAN'S BOOK OF SAINTS.
    A. R. MOWBRAY & CO., LTD.   6/- *net.*

CHURCH HISTORY FROM NERO TO CONSTANTINE.
    A. R. MOWBRAY & CO., LTD.   2/6 *net.*

SHORT HISTORY OF THE CHRISTIAN CHURCH.
    LONGMANS, GREEN & CO., LTD.   10/6 *net.*

SAINTS AND HEROES OF THE CHRISTIAN CHURCH.
    A. R. MOWBRAY & CO., LTD.   2/6 *net.*

THE OXFORD MOVEMENT AND AFTER.
    A. R. MOWBRAY & CO., LTD.   [Out of print].

THE VIA MEDIA

BEING

A VINDICATION OF THE FAITH AND ORDER OF THE CHURCH OF ENGLAND

BY

C. P. S. CLARKE

Archdeacon and Canon Residentiary of Chichester
Examining Chaplain to the Lord Bishop of Chichester
and formerly Lecturer in Church History at the Salisbury
Theological College

With Preface by the
LORD BISHOP OF WINCHESTER

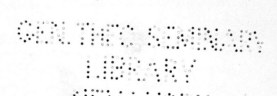
LONGMANS, GREEN AND CO.
LONDON · NEW YORK · TORONTO

LONGMANS, GREEN AND CO. LTD.
39 PATERNOSTER ROW, LONDON, E.C.4
6 OLD COURT HOUSE STREET, CALCUTTA
53 NICOL ROAD, BOMBAY
36A MOUNT ROAD, MADRAS

LONGMANS, GREEN AND CO.
114 FIFTH AVENUE, NEW YORK
221 EAST 20TH STREET, CHICAGO
88 TREMONT STREET, BOSTON

LONGMANS, GREEN AND CO.
215 VICTORIA STREET, TORONTO

First Published 1937

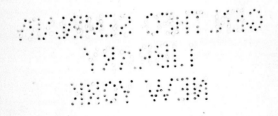

Printed in Great Britain,

To
F. J. H.

PREFACE

I HAVE felt bound to consent to the Archdeacon of Chichester's request that I should
write a preface to this book on the *Via Media*.
Two years ago when he was an incumbent in the
diocese of Winchester, I was discussing with
him his recent book on the history of the Oxford
Movement, and I remember saying to him that I
wished he would write a book stating, in a simple
and straightforward way, the reasons for a loyal
Anglo-Catholic accepting genuinely and whole-
heartedly the position of the Church of England.
This book is a response to that request. In it the
Archdeacon makes it clear why the great majority
of Anglo-Catholics reject the Roman views of
infallibility, authority and private judgment, and
are glad to call themselves true sons and daughters
of the Church of England. Without any bitter-
ness he states the case against Rome and without
any apology the position of his own Church as a
" positive and consistent representation of Christianity—with definite principles of its own."
Against the fundamentalism and authoritarianism
of both Rome and Tennessee he sets the appeal
of the Church of England to the Scriptures, to

the corporate experience of the Church expressed through Creeds and Councils, and to rightly informed private judgment. As I read the book more than once I was reminded of Bishop Creighton's statement that the special characteristic of the Church of England is that it continuously makes its appeal to sound learning.

I know of no recent book which has stated so clearly the *Via Media* in terms which are free from that note of timid deprecation which is sometimes heard from those who recognize but regret that the Church of England is both Catholic and Reformed. The Archdeacon shows moreover that the *Via Media* is something far wider than the Church of England or even Anglicanism. He sums up the argument of his book with the words that " within the providence of God the Church of England rediscovered and in course of time propagated certain principles vital in the life of the Church that were in danger of being forgotten. We do both ourselves and other religious communions, and the sacred cause of charity itself, a real disservice if we belittle our own achievement."

This book should be of real value, and I hope it will be widely read. I do not find myself in agreement with all its author's opinions, but I can whole-heartedly recommend it as a well-balanced and carefully considered statement of the distinctive position of the Church of England as held by a loyal son of the Oxford Movement. I would especially commend it to those who are either Romeward drawn or who are inclined to look upon the *Via Media* as an euphemism for weak compromise. The book should confirm and justify their allegiance to the Church of England.

CYRIL WINTON.

October 1936.

NOTE

I WISH to express my grateful thanks to my friends the Bishop of Brechin, the Dean of Chichester, the Rev. Lancelot Mason, Dr. Dorothy Meads and Mr. C. H. Blakiston, who have read the whole or part of this work in typescript, and have given me both criticism and encouragement, though they have no responsibility for anything in it. Above all I wish to thank the Bishop of Winchester for writing the Preface.

I HAVE consulted many books and am under an obligation to many authors, which I have acknowledged when I could. But I feel I owe a special debt to Professor N. P. Williams' Essay, *The Theology of the Oxford Movement* in *Northern Catholicism*, which I hereby gratefully acknowledge.

C. P. S. CLARKE.

The Chantry,
    Chichester.
        December 1936.

CONTENTS

xi

" The Lot is fallen unto me in a fair ground :
yea, I have a goodly heritage." Ps. 16⁷

CHAPTER I

PROLOGUE

"It is always unwise to speak of a 'system' of Christian doctrine, as though it were something complete, settled and unified—like a railway time-table or nautical almanac. It is a complexity, even a *complexio oppositorum*—a complexity of contradictions. It is perpetual tension. Yet its very complexity gives it a tonic quality, which no mere system could possess. A system satisfies second-rate minds alone. It does indeed offer them a kind of contentment, but it is a stagnant contentment at best. But a complete paradox calls forth vital energy from minds of the highest order, intent if not upon resolving the paradox—at least upon penetrating deeper and deeper still into its mysteries of hidden truth."—

K. E. KIRK, *The Crisis of Christian Rationalism*.

"NO man can justly blame me," wrote Archbishop Bramhall in a passage quoted by Newman, "for honouring my spiritual Mother the Church of England, in whose womb I was conceived, at whose breasts I was nourished, and in whose bosom I hope to die. Bees, by

1

B

the instinct of nature, do love their hives, and birds their nests."[1]

These words strike an answering chord in many breasts. But to strike an answering chord is not enough. We, who aspire, in however humble a degree, to be teachers, must be able to give a reason for the faith that is in us, and to give an answer not only to the enemy in the gate but to those of our brethren who have lost faith in their own Church, and regard it as something to be apologized for, and kept in the background as much as possible, a barely tolerable halting place on the road to Rome, or some form of Protestantism; who share the defeatist spirit of Newman when he wrote with such despairing rhetoric; "We are not better than our fathers; let us bear to be what Hammond was, or Andrews, or Hooker; let us not faint under that body of death, which they bore about with patience; nor shrink from the penalty of sins which they inherited from the age before them."

It is of course perfectly true that the Church of England since the Reformation has much to repent of, as, indeed, it had before that cataclysm came about. But if it comes to that, which of

---

[1] *A Replication to the Bishop of Chalcedon's Survey of the Vindication of the Church of England.* Part I, Discourse iii.

the several fragments of Christendom has not ? We all need a garb of sackcloth at appropriate times, but I refuse to admit that for the English Church to-day, or the Churches in communion with her, sackcloth is the only wear. " The vacillation of a Cranmer," writes Dr. Alington[1] with perfect truth, " and the sins of Henry VIII are innocent compared to the iniquities of the mediæval papacy, and few would deny that the shame for the sins of Protestantism must at least be shared with those whose conduct provoked it."[2]

The *Via Media* was a much bigger thing than the Church of England even a century ago, a fact which Newman wilfully disregarded, when he allowed himself to be carried away by the thought that the Anglo-Catholic idea of the Church had never existed in fact, but only in imagination. " Protestantism and Popery," he sadly wrote, " are real religions :—but the *Via Media* has never existed except on paper ; it has never been reduced to practice." " What is this," he sighed, " but to fancy a road over mountains and rivers, which has never been cut ! "

[1] *Things Ancient and Modern.*

[2] *Lectures on the Prophetical Office of the Church, viewed relatively to Romanism and Popular Protestantism,* afterwards republished together with some miscellaneous Essays under the title of *The Via Media of the Church of England.*

Newman, however, ignored the Anglo-Catholic Churches in Scotland and America, and the Church of the Caroline divines and the Non-Jurors. He had possibly never heard of the Dutch Old Catholics, but why does he treat the Eastern Church as though it did not exist? Whether Orthodox and Old Catholics would own the name of *Via Media* I cannot say, but they certainly come between Popery and Protestantism. But both in Scotland and in the United States of America a Non-Roman episcopal Church had survived a long persecution, in either case so protracted and so severe that the Church could hardly have survived if it had stood for a mere negation.

Since Newman wrote the sentence quoted above, the Churches of the *Via Media* outside England have increased enormously. Not only among English-speaking races throughout the world but in India, China, and Japan the *Via Media* is to be found as a working system. It is reasonable, then, to assume that it is no mere halting place between Rome and Protestantism, but " a positive and consistent representation of Christianity with definite principles of its own," and that it witnesses to principles of vital importance that but for it might be trodden under foot. If there are no such principles, the Church of England and the Churches in communion with her have no right to perpetuate schism by making this third party the *Via Media* between the two extremes, Roman Catholics and Non-episcopal Protestants.

The question to-day has a special urgency. For the need of reunion is being pressed on the minds and consciences of Christendom. On the one hand there is the Church of Rome impressive with its unyielding claim to be the mother and mistress of all Churches, insisting that there can be no reunion without submission. On the other a vast mass of Protestants, with many fissiparous tendencies, anything but homogeneous, but still recognizable as a definite class of Christians who disclaim the name of Catholic and have in a great measure cut themselves adrift from historic Christianity. If there is no great principle involved should we not rather make haste, some to submit to Rome, the rest to join whatever Protestant body takes their fancy, instead of hugging our isolation. There would at least, it might appear, be one schism the less. If not, on what principle do we take our stand? What is there to justify our standing apart from one or other of the groups?

If it were only a question of the Church of England some people might put forward the principle of Establishment as justifying separation. They might urge the age-long connexion with the State going back to the days of the Witan and the Saxon kings, a connexion unbroken except during the Protectorate for 1300 years ; the high character and ability of its Bishops ; its visible consecration of the secular activities of the State ; its provision of spiritual ministrations, to all and sundry. These are important assets, but they do not of themselves justify acquiescence in disunion, while many regard this State connexion as a liability rather than an asset. But the *Via Media* is much bigger than the Church of England.

Again the principle of nationalism has been invoked to justify separation, by which is meant that as the Church of England is the Church of the English nation, so *Nippon Seikokwei* is the Church of the Japanese nation, and both witness to the rights of nationalism in religion. National feeling is such a deep-seated part of human nature that nationalism in the Church, the right that is to a great measure of national autonomy in ritual, ceremonial, and discipline, seems to belong to the rightful liberty of the children of God, but nationalism is not, and never can be, a fundamental principle on which the Church can be built. The reason is partly that in every nation the Church is only part of the nation, and partly because the sentiment of nationalism is becoming discredited; unregulated nationalism is a curse in the modern world, and it must be the function of the Church to transcend the barriers of nationality, not to strengthen them. It is an undoubted strength of the Roman Church that it does in a measure so transcend these barriers and, in the present state of the world, we want a Church that will succeed in doing this more, not less. It is, in fact, a weakness of the Church of England that it has been so much identified, at least in England, with this principle of nationalism.

What, then, is the principle that justifies the separate existence of these non-Roman Churches, which claim to be Catholic? Is there in fact, as Professor N. P. Williams has asserted, a Catholicism which is non-Roman? I maintain that there is such a principle and that it is to be found in a working synthesis between those two opposites authority and freedom, which we look for in vain either in the Roman Church or in the various non-Episcopal communions.

Mr. Gladstone in the year 1869, when he was Prime Minister, declared in a letter to Cardinal

Manning, that "the master-hope, the master passion" of his soul, was to devote the remainder of his life to a reconciliation between Christianity and the conditions of modern thought. He complained that thirty years before Lord Macaulay had covered him with "unqualified and glittering ridicule" because he had professed his allegiance to two principles, "authority and freedom." "After thirty years of the blasts of life, I remain," he said, "rooted as much as before, in regard for authority, and even more than before in the value I set upon freedom. It has pleased God at a heavy cost to give it (freedom) the place of a foundation-stone in the being of man—under no inducement whatever could I without treason to duty, consent whether in religion or in secular affairs to its being trodden under foot."

These principles managed to exist side by side in the early Church, until it was swamped by the hordes of ignorant barbarians in the fifth and sixth centuries who were baptized *en masse* without instruction or preparation worth the name. For centuries it was the business of the Church to induce these neophytes and their descendants to believe what they were told and do as they were bid. Freedom was not for them. Voices were occasionally heard in protest, of which that of Peter Abelard was the loudest, but authority, almost undiluted, reigned without serious challenge until the Reformation. As education spread, a minority became less docile, the Church had to call in the secular arm to reinforce spiritual authority with fire and sword, and a gigantic system of espionage was set up by the Inquisition, which was founded in 1233. The Reformation was in part a revolt against authority and the assertion of individual freedom, and was rendered inevitable by what had gone before.

Wicliffe has some times been called the Morning Star of the Reformation, the Morning Star being that luminary which immediately precedes the dawn. Erasmus might with better reason be called the Morning Star of the *Via Media*. He does not always appear in a heroic light, and he certainly had no love for martyrdom, but over and above his great services to learning he spent his life in fighting the obscurantism, the tyranny, and the abuses of the mediæval church on the one hand, and the violence and destructiveness of the Reformers on the other. In his reasonableness, his belief in discussion, and his appeal to learning and the example of the primitive Church, he was a true forerunner of the *Via Media*.

The principles of the *Via Media* in the West

first found, or rather refound, concrete expression in the Church of England. They have since spread all over the world and continue to spread. It is the purpose of this book to elucidate these principles and commend them specially to the country of their rebirth, where their importance is in some quarters in danger of being forgotten.

CHAPTER II

AUTHORITY

" It seems that whether in a medicine man cluttered up with fetiches and gauds, or at Delphi, or at Rome, or in a book on the parlour table, or in a laboratory, or a ' Grouper ' notebook, man wants an infallible voice that shall tell him emphatically and clearly what he must believe. In turn each of his oracles fails. The mumbling of the medicine man is fast sinking into silence in the vanishing fastnesses of the primeval forests ; the grove of Apollo is forsaken beyond repair, Rome's thundering infallibility trembles before even more loudly mouthed dictators, and the dust accumulates upon the Bible in the parlour. The nineteenth century supposed fondly that Science was ready to take the vacant throne only, as the century died, to hear disappointedly the voice failing and the confident ring of ' Scientia locuta est ' giving place to the more diffident tones of the modern seeker after truth."

Jack, Jill and God, by R. A. EDWARDS, p. 89.

IT is perfectly plain that there must be authority in the apprehension of Christianity, because it claims to be a revealed religion, and a revealed religion as its name implies has in it something which we could not discover for ourselves which has accordingly to be shown and revealed. It has in it, therefore, an element of *given-ness*. We receive it, in the first place, because it is revealed. To say that a truth is revealed is to say that we take it in the first place on authority.

Now it is obvious that even in the acquisition of knowledge concerning this world we have to take a good deal on authority. We accept the theory of evolution, for instance, and the Copernican system on authority in the first place, at least as working hypotheses. In the same way the young Christian has to begin by accepting certain truths about the supernatural, as the young biologist or astronomer has to take on authority facts of the natural world. He must accept them first, at least as working hypotheses, and investigate afterwards.

It is plain that the Christian religion is revealed. We did not discover it. Christ came and revealed Himself. His Apostles believed in Him and in their turn they passed on as well as they could what they had learned. The Church has existed ever since to bear its witness to this knowledge. Its very *raison d'être* is its possession of the knowledge of God. If God had never

spoken in this way there is an end of all the claims
of any positive religion on the universal allegiance
of mankind. For, left to our own unaided
efforts, the results we shall arrive at would be so
divergent that we should conclude that they
were of no great importance. We have only to
imagine the extraordinarily divergent conclusions
a dozen intelligent men and women would arrive
at, if they came with open minds to discover what
the true religion is, with the help of such evidence
as is afforded by the Bible regarded purely as a
collection of historical records, by the external
aspect of nature, by the science of comparative
religion, and by biology. Even so they would
have to take most of the evidence second-hand,
that is *on authority*, for no human brain could have
a first-hand knowledge of all the subjects which
would have to be taken into consideration.
We must have something more positive if we
profess a religion which claims to be world-wide.
Otherwise we cannot go to all nations and say,
" This is the way. Walk ye in it."

It has been said with truth that we can never
discard authority, we can only choose our masters.[1]

It is worth noticing—Professor Taylor brings
it out—that an unusual awareness of authority

[1] *The Faith of a Moralist.*

has marked every great religious revival. The Apostles had it. The Jesuits were alike champions of papal authority and the most persistent and enthusiastic missionaries that Christendom has known. They had been evangelizing the heathen for a century and had planted the Cross in all parts of the New World as well as the Old, before the first Protestant missionaries, the Moravian brethren, sailed from Europe. In the Church of England the bodies which have shown most evangelizing zeal have been the Evangelicals and the Anglo-Catholics. The Evangelicals spurred on by their faith in the Bible, as the Word of God verbally inspired by the Holy Ghost, established missionary outposts everywhere abroad. The Anglo-Catholics with their firm belief in the authority of the Church led the van in the conversion of the heathen in our great cities at home. Each alike had a strong belief in authority. One in the authority of the Bible; the other in that of the Church.

Now authority is an ambiguous word. It sometimes means sovereign authority, or supreme ruling power, corresponding to the Latin word *imperium*. But *auctoritas* from which our word authority is derived means properly influence, or weight, used in the sense in which we use it when we say, for example, that so-and-so is an authority on astronomy, or Egyptian hieroglyphics, or the hydrogenization of coal, or whatever his particular subject may be. The authority is not necessarily infallible. It must be supported by reasons. It may be questioned. It may conceivably be mistaken.

But by religious authority people often mean an autocratic and oracular[1] authority, which may not be questioned. When an ancient Greek needed advice he sometimes had recourse to the oracle of Delphi, where he sought advice from a priestess, supposed to be the mouthpiece of the god Apollo. Now this advice might be good, or bad, but was held to be decisive. He might argue about the meaning, but not about the advice itself. The advice was final. He might take it or not, but it was above argument. It was an oracle.

The first question, therefore, to be answered is—"Have Christians such an oracular authority?" Are the assumptions which we take on authority to be received as oracular? or do they lie open freely to our question and debate; must we say " this, an authority, which cannot be

---

[1] For this use of oracular I am indebted to *One God and Father of All*—E. Milner-White and W. Knox.

mistaken, tells us is true, and therefore it is impious to call it in question " ? or, " this is the truth according to an authority of the greatest possible weight. But you are welcome to examine it and see for yourself, whether you believe it to be true. We believe that if you examine it fairly you will agree with it, but you are welcome to inquire, whatever the result. Meantime we commend it as at least a working hypothesis."

If there is an oracular authority in religion we should expect it to be also infallible. It seems absurd to have an authority making oracular pronouncements which must not be disputed or discussed, but which may later on be discarded ; it would be ridiculous to have to believe to-day as a truth necessary to salvation something which to-morrow you may be a heretic for believing.

Our first business then is to discover whether there is such an oracular authority, which we must obey because of its inherent right to obedience and not because its pronouncements may be tested by our reason, our conscience, or our experience.

INFALLIBILITY

The idea of infallibility, of an authority which can give an infallible answer to men and women bewildered by the problems of religion, has great attractions for many who desire an authority which will settle the question in dispute and leave no room for doubt. The prevailing unrest and scepticism in religion produces a desire for assurance. Cardinal Manning more than sixty years ago, seeing that the flood-gates were open and that the world was about to be submerged under a tide of liberal propaganda, demanded that the Infallibility of the Pope should be defined, as a bulwark against infidelity. To-day the flood of anti-Christian books since the war has been answered in part by a revival of belief in the verbal Inspiration of the Bible—Fundamentalism —to give it its common name. Just as the devout Roman Catholic can take refuge under the aegis of the infallible Pope, so the Fundamentalist shelters behind the infallible Word of God in the Bible. The waters rage and the floods surge, but the Roman and the Fundamentalist cling like limpets to their respective rocks.

Belief in infallibility was, indeed, general when the verbal inspiration of the Bible was usually taken for granted. Hugh Miller, for instance, a distinguished Scottish geologist, a Presbyterian, who visited England in 1843, condemned Tractarianism for being without infallibility. " In every form of Christianity in which men are in

earnest," he wrote, " there must be an infallibility somewhere. By the Episcopalian Protestant, or by the Presbyterian, that infallibility is
recognized as resting in the scriptures ; and by the
consistent Papist that infallibility is recognized
as resting in the Church. But where does the
infallibility of the Puseyite rest ? Not in the
Scriptures for repudiating the right of private
judgement he is necessarily ignorant of what the
Scriptures truly teach. Not in tradition for he
has no trustworthy guide to show him where
tradition is right, or where it is wrong. Not in
his Church ; for his Church has no voice ; or rather
—her voice is a gabble of conflicting sounds."
But to-day we cannot assume infallibility. Our
first question must be : " is there any infallible
authority on earth ? "

Against it we might urge first of all that there
is nothing in our knowledge of the natural
world to lead us to expect infallibility in our
knowledge of God. A great many discoveries,
the evolutionary method, for example, and the
Copernican system, are taken for granted by
later workers. But they are open to discussion. In the last resort we believe that the earth
goes round the sun not because Copernicus, or
anyone else, said so, but because the belief that it

does go round the sun fits in with what we know of the heavens. In the same way, though we accept certain dogmas on the authority of the Church and the Bible, and not because we have discovered them for ourselves, we retain our belief in them because they are inherently reasonable, fitting in with what we know of the world, because they appeal to our sense of what is morally right, and because they are corroborated by the experience of our lives, and by our knowledge of history, and finally because, besides all these converging testimonies, a movement of assent springs up within our hearts, which we call faith. The dogma of infallibility dehumanizes religion, making our knowledge of it depend on means which have nothing analogous in our acquisition of knowledge of other things.

Secondly the records of our Lord's life give no indication of infallibility. To begin with, we see that His own knowledge had limitations. " But of that day and that hour knoweth no man," He said, " no, not the angels, which are in heaven, neither the Son, but the Father." " If it be possible," He cried in Gethsemane, " let this cup pass from Me, nevertheless not My will but Thine be done." The cry of desolation on the Cross, " My God, My God, why hast Thou forsaken Me?" also implies a limitation of knowledge. The servant is not above his master. If the Divine Master permitted His knowledge to be limited why should we, His servants, expect to have an infallible source of knowledge at our command?

Again, though as a teacher He is admittedly unique, though He revealed truths His disciples could not have found out for themselves and were therefore bound to accept on His authority, His teaching methods were rather Socratic, that is intended to provoke thought, than oracular, inviting blind acceptance of dogmatic statements. Even when put in their most oracular form— "Moses said—but I say"—their very nature constitutes a challenge. At that day in Palestine the best way to provoke thought and discussion was to balance one oracular statement with another. Moses was accepted by all Jews as an oracle. When Jesus set Himself up as a superior authority He made a challenge. It is certainly remarkable that where He is most oracular in His dogmatic pronouncements, namely on the marriage of divorced persons, there has been no universal agreement as to His meaning.

It is certain that our Lord left no clear-cut theology of God or of His own Person. His followers had to work out one for themselves. The doctrine of the Trinity came to be believed not because it was taught explicitly by our Lord, or even by His Apostles, but because it was a rational inference from various facts which were part of the tradition of the Church. As Tertullian put it there could only be one sovereignty in the Deity, but it was equally clear from the New Testament that the Father, the Son, and the Holy Ghost were each divine. In spite of Peter's confession, it is doubtful if either he or the Apostles had any clear belief that Jesus was God until they made the inference from His words, and acts, and the events of His life, culminating in the Resurrection. All along they were left to make inferences, whereas if infallibility is to be our guide, one should expect plain statements. The Penny Catechism is the natural outcome of an infallible authority. Anything less like the Penny Catechism than our Lord's teaching in the New Testament it is difficult to conceive.

Infallibility, then, in religion, is unlikely both in itself and from what we know of our Lord's teaching and practice in the Gospels.

But apart from what is antecedently likely, or unlikely, what evidence is there to show that infallibility has existed as a fact?

We must first of all consider the claims made so insistently and so aggressively by the Church of Rome for its Head. " We offer you," says Father Woodlock, " successors to Peter, sharing his prerogative that he will never teach false doctrine in matters of faith and conduct, when he solemnly and officially addresses the whole Church as its visible Head, defining and making clear a doctrinal point, or proclaiming it as the Word of God handed over to him and deposited with him at the beginning."[1]

When we come to examine the origin of the claim we find that the case in the gospels rests mainly on the text in St. Matthew. " Thou art Peter and on this rock I will build my Church " : on the command in the fourth gospel—" Feed my sheep, . . . Feed my lambs ": and on the charge in St. Luke's gospel—" When thou art converted, strengthen thy brethren."

Two of the texts do not seem to amount to very much. The charge to strengthen his brethren was uttered at the same time as the prediction of the denial, and contained the warning of His fall and the promise of restoration. The charge to feed Christ's sheep and lambs was given as a sign of restoration after the denial. Both

[1] *Constantinople, Canterbury and Rome.*

charges were meant to afford Peter the hope and promise of reparation ; they find a parallel in Paul's words that he was the least of the Apostles and not worthy to be called an Apostle because he had persecuted the Church and yet had laboured more abundantly than they all.

The text in St. Matthew stands on a different footing. It does give a special position to Peter, which no Anglo-Catholic is concerned to deny. But to build a theology on a single text is most precarious. If the preceding statement of Peter's confession " Thou art the Christ the Son of the living God " : appeared only in Matthew, and there was no other evidence of any account in the whole of the New Testament that our Lord was more than man—how could we believe in His divine claims ?

The authors of Mark and Luke while recording the incident and St. Peter's confession which evoked the promise, omit all mention of the promise itself, which is, to say the least, odd, if the words were meant to have the doctrinal importance afterwards assigned to them.

Mark was the earliest gospel and is believed to have been derived from St. Peter himself. He could not have omitted the words through ignorance. Are we to suppose he omitted them in deference to St. Peter's modesty ? But one does not suppress a vital truth to spare the blushes even of an Apostle.[1] St. Luke, also, ignores the words. The most ardent papalist would hardly suggest that he omits them out of jealousy for his master, St. Paul. The only possible explanation on the papal hypothesis is that St. Mark and St. Luke did not realize the importance of the words ; this is no doubt true. We may go further and say that St. Peter himself shows no sign anywhere in the New Testament that he understood that through them he had received special authority and power. The authority claimed is so tremendous that if St. Peter had held it he and his contemporaries must have been aware of it.

As against the Petrine claims we note that no one of the Apostles was to be called Lord and Master, that all alike received the commission to remit sins. " He breathed on *them* (not him) and *they* received the Holy Ghost " ; that all alike were to sit on twelve thrones judging the twelve tribes of Israel. The promise that the Holy Ghost should guide into all truth is given to *you* (plural) and not to St. Peter alone. St. Peter

[1] The late Professor C. H. Turner thinks they must have come in the lost ending of the gospel ; surely a precarious support for the edifice erected on it.

holds a position of primacy, not supremacy. After the rise of Paul even his primacy is doubtful. After Pentecost Peter is obviously the spokesman and preacher of the little band, but the first constitutional innovation, the appointment of the seven we are told is definitely at the instance of the twelve. " The twelve called the multitude of the disciples," and when the disciples chose the seven " the apostles " laid their hands on them. St. Peter is not mentioned by name.

In the very early days of the Church a question as divisive and critical as ever troubled it afterwards, threatened it with disruption. Gentiles were coming into the Church and the question arose : " Were they to be treated like Jews and be circumcised, and keep the Jewish law, or were they to be free ? " Feeling ran high and the question was referred to Jerusalem for settlement. Here, if ever, was the opportunity for St. Peter to give an infallible judgement. What happened ? First of all St. Paul and St. Barnabas and the rest of the deputation from Antioch " were received of the Church and the Apostles and elders and rehearsed all things that God had done with them."

There is no special mention of St. Peter. After this report the Apostles and elders were apparently

satisfied.   But some Christians, " of the sect
of the Pharisees " persisted in their opposition,
saying, " It is needful to circumcise them and to
keep the law of Moses."   As a result the first
Church Council, of which we have any record,
was summoned.   " The Apostles and elders
were gathered together to consider of this matter,"
constituting the Council.   Again there is no
mention of St. Peter.   The laity were present
but did not speak.   " All the multitude kept
silence."

St. Peter opened the proceedings with a plea
for liberty.   It was in a sense a speech for the
defence, since the conduct of St. Paul and St.
Barnabas and of the Church of Antioch was being
called in question.   Then St. Paul and St.
Barnabas give their evidence, " rehearsing what
signs and orders God had wrought amongst the
Gentiles by them."   Silence followed.   " After
they had held their peace," St. James summed
up and delivered judgement.   " Wherefore my
judgement is that we trouble not them which
from among the Gentiles turn to God."   Could
anything be clearer ?   If there is an infallible
authority anywhere it is James not Peter.   After
the Council we read : " it seemed good to the
Apostles and Elders," with the assent of the whole

Church, to send a deputation to Antioch—not a word about St. Peter—with a letter beginning—" The Apostles and the Elders," and ending " It seemed good to the Holy Ghost and to us to lay upon you no greater burden."

Now no one denies that St. Peter is prominent at the Council. Inevitably. He was the leader and spokesman of the apostles. St. Paul and St. Barnabas were in comparison upstarts, especially St. Paul. They were accused of false teaching by the ultra-conservatives. If unity was to be preserved it was necessary that one of the original apostles who possessed the confidence of the conservatives should champion their cause, and St. Peter as the spokesman and leader of the apostolic band, who had himself received the vision which led to the baptism of Cornelius, was the obvious person to do it, and so to bridge the gap which threatened to become a chasm. But it is plain that St. James is the president and delivers judgement. It seems equally plain that if he, or St. Peter, or anyone else, had known that St. Peter was divinely inspired to deliver an oracular judgement this would have been the occasion for its delivery.

The doctrine of development does not cover the discrepancy between the situation we find

here and the claims made later for the Papacy.
The gulf between the spokesman of the apostolic
band, as we find him in the New Testament, and
the Pope as the divinely commissioned autocrat
and infallibly inspired oracle is so tremendous that
no doctrine of development will span it.   There
is not even the embryo of the doctrine in the
New Testament.

If there is an infallible oracle it is St. Paul,
who is a far more dominant person than St.
Peter.   It is interesting to note that where
Father Woodlock wishes to illustrate the dogmatic and positive attitude of the early Church
as opposed to the right of private judgement
claimed by Bishop Gore, he illustrates his
thesis from the Epistles of St. Paul.   " Does St.
Paul," he asks, " show himself adverse to the
dogmatizing method and mere submissiveness
to authority ?   He talks in the tone of a Roman
Pope anathematizing a Modernist."   I am not
concerned to defend St. Paul's methods but how
much better for Father Woodlock's argument
if he had been able to quote St. Peter instead of
St. Paul !   It is strange that the only Apostle
whose utterance can be quoted as resembling a
modern Pope denouncing a Modernist is St.
Paul.   Not, perhaps, so much because of the

argument from the silence of Peter, but because if there were an infallible authority in the background, even the germ of one, we should not expect to find subordinate authority, anathematizing, dogmatizing, laying down the law, and even rebuking his superior.

Even if Peter possessed the gift of infallibility we have no knowledge that he transmitted the gift to the Pope. There is no proof that Peter was ever *Bishop* of Rome. The earliest writers, Clement, Ignatius and Irenaeus speak of Peter and Paul as *joint founders* of the Roman Church and say that they instituted Linus as the first *Bishop*. The belief that Peter was the first Bishop of Rome, originated in the pseudo-Clementine writings, religious romances which were fathered on Clement of Rome and passed as his work for many centuries. The Epistle to James the Lord's brother which contains the statement that Peter, when Bishop of Rome, appointed Clement as his successor can according to Lightfoot " hardly be earlier than the middle of the second century or much later than the beginning of the third." As history it is worthless.

We find no evidence of the recognition of papal infallibility in the ante-Nicean Church. It was torn by controversy over the date of Easter, over the re-admission to communion of those who had sacrificed in time of persecution, over heretical baptism. Passions ran high. In more than one instance the advice of the Bishop of Rome is sought but in no single case does anyone act as if he knew that the Bishop of Rome could give an inspired and final opinion.

When Irenaeus in his controversy with the Gnostics had to meet their claim that they possessed a secret tradition descended from the Apostles, he challenged them to set their secret tradition against the tradition of the Churches founded by the Apostles. In every such Church there was, he maintains, a succession of Bishops from the Apostle founders, who would have handed on from one to another any secret tradition if there had been such a thing. Instead of proving his point by enumerating all the successions of Bishops in every Church founded by an Apostle, he takes one such Church as sufficient for an example, namely, the Church of Rome, " for to this Church on account of its superior pre-eminence, it must needs be that all Churches come together, that is, the faithful from all sides ; and in this Church the Tradition from the Apostles has been always preserved " (not as elsewhere by a merely local body) " by men from all parts."[1]

This passage is a great papalist text. Here, they say, you see a plain proof that by the year 170 A.D. or thereabouts, if there is any doubt as to the orthodoxy of any particular doctrine you must consult the Church of Rome. But consider the matter a little further. Why must you consult the Church of Rome? Because its Bishop is an infallible Pope and can give you an infallible answer? Not at all. On the other hand, it is because the Church of Rome by reason of its position is the resort of Christians belonging to all other churches founded by Apostles and therefore, if it had deviated by ever so little from the Apostolic traditions, some of these strangers would set it right. If the Bishop of Rome had been recognized as infallible, his infallibility would have been the ground, the entirely sufficient ground, for appealing to his authority. Why bring in the other Apostolic Churches as guarantors of the orthodoxy of Rome if its Bishop was infallible?

In the post-Nicene period when the chief

---

[1] Bishop Gore's translation. The passage is much disputed, as an alternative translation for *come together* is *agree*: this translation, however, does violence to the context.

dogmas of the Church were defined the method was definitely conciliar not papal. The great Councils of Nicea and Constantinople, produced our Nicene Creed. The Councils of Ephesus and Chalcedon further defined the nature of Christ. It is true that at Chalcedon the Council accepted the Tome of Leo I, but the authority came from the Council rather than the Pope, and is not therefore accepted by all Roman theologians as an infallible utterance.

The final objection to papal infallibility is a practical one. No one knows when the Pope speaks infallibly. When Cardinal Manning worked so hard to get the Infallibility definition made part of necessary doctrine he believed that it would be a serviceable weapon against the advancing hosts of Liberalism, because he thought that every official utterance of the papacy would be stronger if it possessed the hall-mark of infallibility. " The practical importance of this question of Papal Infallibility," Manning wrote in 1869 before the Vatican Council met, " will be manifest at once by remembering that for three hundred years the Pontiffs have elaborated and expressly considered a long series of propositions in theology and philosophy. The THESES DAMNATAE are very numerous. Now are these fallible or infallible ? Do they require of us the assent of faith, resting upon the Divine authority from which they emanate, or are they venerable utterances, " to be respected, indeed, always, with assent if we agree with them, and with silence if we do not ? Has the Church then for three hundred years been mistaking doubtful utterances for certainties, and that in matters of faith and morality involving the absolution of souls from sin ? They who deny the infallibility of the Pontiffs have a hard task to reconcile this theory with fidelity to conscience and truth."

The letter went on to explain the scope of infallibility. It included "all dogmatic judgements" and dogmatic judgements embraced all judgements in matters of dogma such as " the inspiration and authority of sacred books, the orthodoxy or heterodoxy of human and uninspired books," and the grammatical and literal sense of texts. Infallibility was also to rest upon papal judgements referring to " laws of discipline, canonization of saints, approbation of religious orders, of devotions and the like." Manning, in fact, correctly judged that unless infallibility covered all formal dogmatic decisions it would not amount to much.

But for practical purposes it is as though the

D

doctrine had never been defined, because no one knows whether any particular utterance is infallible, or not. Was that decree of Infallibility infallible? No one knows. Pope Leo XIII in 1896 issued a decree condemning Anglican Orders addressed to all the Bishops of the Christian Church in East and West. Was that infallible? Some say one thing; some another. In 1907 Pius X issued his famous Bull, *Pastor Gregis*, condemning modernism. Is that infallible? No one knows. Or, perhaps, it would be more correct to say that a great many Roman authorities know, but their opinions do not agree. Pius X in the *Ne Temere* decree revoked the age-long practice of the Church by declaring marriages between Catholics and non-Catholics no marriage unless covered by a dispensation. The present Pope not long ago issued a message to the civilized world in which he made many grave pronouncements on matters of sexual morality, and condemned the use of contraceptives as mortal sin. Are these infallible judgements or pious opinions? The only papal utterance the infallibility of which seems to command universal assent is the Bull decreeing the Immaculate Conception of our Lady (1854).

Father Woodlock urges Anglo-Catholics to

join " a Church which teaches clearly, authoritatively, infallibly, ' all the things ' whatsoever Christ has heard from the Father." No one denies that his Church teaches clearly and authoritatively but neither Father Woodlock nor any one else knows when she speaks infallibly.

But in point of fact the distinction between infallible and non-infallible papal utterances is unreal, because for practical purposes papal utterances have to be treated as though they were infallible. " Surely in real life," wrote Cardinal Merry del Val, " and so far as the practical conduct of men is concerned, to be free from error and to be above all possible accusation of error, come practically to one and the same thing."[1] Now Rome had claimed for centuries before Infallibility had been made *de fide* that the official utterances of the Pope were " above all possible accusation of error," or, in other words oracular, and this claim continues now that infallibility having been defined turns out to be a letter, which if not dead, is at least inoperative. It is the assumption that to every question there must be an answer, which Rome can give, and that every official answer must be treated as infallible, or at least as sacrosanct, until withdrawn by a

[1] *The Truth of Papal Claims*, p. 21.

later utterance of the same authority. Now the only justification for such a system is infallibility. If the oracle is divinely inspired and must be right, it is no good to discuss, to argue, or to refute. But for the oracle to give utterances which may be mistaken but are nevertheless always to be received " with assent if we agree with them and with silence if we do not " is to stifle inquiring minds and to bandage the eyes of the earnest seeker.

When we find that papal utterances, however formal and official, are sometimes mistaken, and even contradictory, we fail to see why the Pope in uttering them should be regarded as divinely inspired or immune from judgement at the bar of the reason, the conscience, and the experience of mankind.

Pope Honorius (625–638), for instance, in 634 sent a letter to Sergius, Patriarch of Constantinople, approving of the Monothelite doctrine, which that Prelate had set forth. This letter was a formal and official document. On account of it the Sixth Oecumenical Synod, which met at Constantinople in 680, condemned him as a heretic as did also his successor Leo II who wrote in a letter to the Emperor : " We equally anathematize the inventors of the new error (here follows a list of names) and *Honorius*, who did not

illuminate this Apostolic Church with the doctrine
of Apostolic tradition, but by profane teaching
endeavoured to subvert its spotless Faith." And
in a letter to Spanish Bishops[1] he declared that
Honorius with other heretics had been punished
with eternal condemnation.

To take another instance. For many years the
Franciscan Order was rent with a controversy, as
to whether the rule of St. Francis was to be
obeyed literally or not. The Spiritual Franciscans
championed the literal observance, the Conventual
Franciscans the laxer interpretation of the Rule.
After fifty years of strife both parties appealed to
Pope Gregory X who decided in favour of the
Spirituals. The quarrel, however, continued,
becoming more and more envenomed, until in
1279 Pope Nicholas III undertook to settle it
with a formal decision. After devoting two
months to the study of the question with the
assistance of two Franciscan Cardinals, the
General of the Order, and some of its Provincials,
he submitted their conclusions to a Commission,
which included Benedetto Caietano, the future
Pope Boniface VIII. With their deliberations to
guide him he came to a decision and read it in
full consistory ; he then issued it to the world,

---

[1] Mansi XI, 1052.

in a Bull known to history as *Exiit qui seminet* (the sower went forth to sow). His judgement was included twenty years later in the additions to the canon law compiled and edited by Pope Boniface VIII. It is difficult to conceive how any utterance on faith and morals could have been sent into the world more formally, or claiming higher authority, or more fully complying with the conditions laid down as necessary for infallibility. It was a decision in favour of the Spiritual Franciscans, and declared the Franciscan Rule to be the inspiration of the Holy Ghost. Absolute renunciation of property, it declared, was laudable, and holy, and had been practised by Christ and His Apostles.

But in 1332 Pope John XXII issued the Bull *Cum inter Nonnullos* in which he laid down that it was heresy to deny that Christ and His Apostles held property. In other words, he declared the Bull *Exiit qui seminet* to be heretical; besides its author, his two predecessors, Boniface VIII and Clement V were involved in the same heresy. The Bull was no *brutum fulmen*. A large number of Franciscans were burnt, according to some authorities over a hundred, for maintaining the teaching of a Bull issued by a Pope and accepted by two of his successors.

The working of non-infallible papal authority to define questions of faith and morals is well illustrated in dealing with Biblical criticism. At one time it seemed as if the Roman Church would at least allow the non-literal theory of inspiration. Cardinal Newman in 1884 commenting on the sentence of the Vatican Council that the Scriptures " have God for their author " explained " author " as only meaning " primary cause." A Roman layman, St. George Mivart, published in July and December 1887 articles in which he claimed the right to accept the conclusions of advanced critics. A French periodical was published, *L'Enseignement Biblique*, which dealt with questions of higher criticism. But the obscurantists had their way. Mivart was excommunicated, *L'Enseignement Biblique* suppressed, and a Papal Encyclical *On the Study of Holy Scripture* appeared in 1893, condemning all theories of inspiration except the Fundamentalist.

In 1906 there appeared with the Pope's approbation the Answers of the Pontifical Biblical Commission, which attributed the authorship of the Pentateuch to Moses, and dismissed summarily the whole fabric built up by half a century of scholarship and research. The late Baron von

Hugel, a devout Roman Catholic, thus commented on the Answers.

" The opinion of the Biblical Commission is surely but one link in a chain of official attempts at the suppression, or emasculation, of science and scholarship beginning, indeed, with Erasmus and culminating with Richard Simon and Alfred Loisy, but never entirely absent as witness countless workers' lives well known to their fellow-workers. When and where has Rome abandoned any position however informal and late its occupation and however undemonstrated its tenableness ? Where in particular is the case of its permission to hold critical and historical views even distantly comparable in their deviation from tradition to those here presented to us ? And if no such cases can be found then surely Rome stands utterly discredited."

He went on, however, to plead that the Commission's answer was not a dogmatic decision and might be reversed. Far from reversing it the Pope issued in 1907 the Bull *Lamentalili exitu* in which a number of propositions were condemned as heretical, including the statement that " Divine Inspiration is not extended to Holy Scripture in such a way as to preserve the whole, or each part, from mistake." God is declared to be the author of Holy Scripture in the sense that any error in the text would involve " that God Himself was deceived." No Roman Catholic may deny the Mosaic authorship of the first five books of the Bible, nor teach that the first three chapters of Genesis are not literal history, nor that St. Mark's gospel was written first and St. Matthew's afterwards, nor question that the Epistle to the Hebrews was written by St. Paul.

Again in its attitude to persecution, or the use of physical force to promote spiritual ends, official Roman, that is papal, doctrine outrages the conscience as its official doctrine on Biblical criticism does the intellect. Innocent III inaugurated the use of fire and sword on the grand scale in his sermon at his enthronement in 1198 when he called upon Christian princes to extirpate the *Albigensian* heretics. During the following century the Popes launched Crusade after Crusade not only against the infidel but to enforce orthodoxy and to uphold their own autocracy. Raynaldi, an Oratorian " distinguished for his piety and benevolence,"[1] records with approval that the Archbishop of Narbonne in 1243 " strenuously carrying out the apostolic commands" (i.e., of Innocent IV) delivered more than

[1] *Catholic Encyclopædia*

two hundred heretics of either sex to the flames. In 1233 Gregory IX had set up the Inquisition and so established a regular machinery of persecution which endeavoured to coerce the consciences of mankind, wherever it could get a footing, in the New World as well as the old, for a period of six hundred years. Blanco White (b. 1775) records in his Autobiography that he actually witnessed an *auto-da-fé* in Spain. The victim was a woman, and though a reprieve arrived at the last minute, she died of shock.

Now all this policy of persecution was definitely papal. " The Popes," wrote Lord Acton, himself a Roman Catholic,[1] "were individually and collectively responsible for persecution in the thirteenth and fourteenth centuries and for the Spanish Inquisition." Nor has the leopard changed his spots.[2] Pius IX in 1864 condemned the teaching that " the Church has no right to coerce by temporal penalties those who transgress Christ's

---

[1] *Historical Essays and Studies*, p. 505.

[2] " Ecclesiastical rulers may punish with the sword, if they can, and if it is expedient and necessary to do so. . . . Is not the miraculous infliction of judgments upon blasphemy, lying, profaneness, etc., in the apostles' day a sanction of the infliction of the same by a human hand in the times of the Inquisition ? The Church has a right to make laws and to enforce these with temporal penalties." Cardinal Newman. Quoted by Lord Acton, *The History of Freedom and Other Essays*, p. 425.

laws." " The Pope," wrote a keen observer in 1869, " would like to have freedom of conscience in Serbia and Russia, but only as a means which may be used to propagate truth in those countries."[1] " The Pope and Monsignor Pie were agreed that only in countries where Catholics were in a minority might religious freedom be wished for by Catholics."[2] In the *Catholic Encyclopædia* the right to use coercion is upheld.

In view then of the inconsistency of papal utterances on official and weighty occasions, of their denial of the rights of the human reason in the case of Biblical criticism, and of the conscience in the case of persecution, there is something ironical in Father Woodlock's confident assertion! " One teacher alone has Christ's voice of authority. The Church of Peter to-day is the only dogmatic teacher of truth." When he says, alluding to the Roman Church, " He that heareth you, heareth me," he seems to make our Lord sanction the whole bloody system of persecution and wars of religion, which has caused oceans of blood to be shed in the name of Him, Who when the sons of Zebedee wished to rain down fire from heaven to consume the Samaritans replied—" Ye know not what spirit ye are of. The

---

[1] Nielsen, *Hist. Papacy in Nineteenth Century*.　　[2] *Ibid.*

Son of Man came not to destroy men's lives but
to save them."

The oracular authority of Rome stands self-
condemned.

Infallibility of the Church.

But though we reject the infallibility of the
Pope we may still hold that the Church itself is
infallible, as does the Orthodox Church of the
East. The practical difficulty at once arises,
if we grant the possession of infallibility, as to
how the infallible church is to speak, and what is
its organ of expression? The difficulty provides
our Roman Catholic friends with an obvious
point. If the Church is infallible it must have a
voice, or infallibility is ineffective, and if a voice
then a Head to give the voice utterance.

There was in the late Middle Ages a movement
to make General Councils supreme over the Pope
and to find in their decisions that infallibility
which was denied to him. But no student of history can attribute infallibility to the decisions of
General Councils in themselves. The Councils of
Ariminum and Seleucia for example, which met
A.D. 359, adopted compromising decisions on the
divinity of our Lord, which were afterwards
rejected. What is known as the Robber Council

of Ephesus was convoked in 449 as a General
Council. The authority of a General Council
does, in fact, depend not on its constitution but
on the subsequent acceptance of its decisions by
the Church. This has always been the theory of
the Eastern Church, which holds that the Church
itself is infallible, but distinguishes between the
possession of the truth which is the prerogative of
the Church, and its *proclamation*, which belongs to
General Councils. It holds that their decisions
are not in *themselves* infallible, but depend for
infallibility on their subsequent reception by the
Church. This theory gets rid of the oracular
answer, as it leaves room for argument, discussion, the interplay of reasoning, and the gradual
guidance of the Holy Spirit.

It must be remembered that the changes which
have turned the West upside down have hardly
touched the East. The Reformation did not
affect it. The age of reason which in the West
began towards the end of the seventeenth century
passed it by. Scientific discoveries, like the
theory of Evolution and the criticism of the
Bible, have left it unmoved. But the general
ethos of orthodoxy is to trust to tradition, by
which is meant not so much what we call tradition, that is the deposit handed down from the

past, as the general feeling and sentiment of the living church. Believing that the Holy Spirit guides the Church into truth, it trusts to what it calls its *living tradition*. So far, owing to its special conditions this *living tradition* has been intensely conservative. When the thaw comes and the ice melts, there seems no absolute reason why the Orthodox Church should regard the canons of the Church as irreformable.

The English Church is certainly not tied to any belief in the infallibility of General Councils. The 21st Article declares that " they may err and sometimes have erred, even in things pertaining unto God." William Laud, Archbishop of Canterbury (1633–1645), held that General Councils may err, though he thought that they ought to be obeyed until their decisions were revised by another Council, unless they were plainly contrary to scripture. In support of this last contention he quoted a canon of the Council of Constance forbidding communion in both kinds.

The Tractarian Position.

The Tractarians were in a state of lively reaction from the Liberal and Evangelical principle of private judgement. They, like Hugh Miller, and nearly every one else at that day, were inclined to believe that there must be an infallibility somewhere, though they did not believe that it resided either in scripture as interpreted by the private judgements of individuals, or in the Pope. They therefore looked for their authority in the voice of the undivided Church.

" The only way of finding out the meaning of Scripture," wrote Newman, " is to see how the early Church understood it. This is the Anglican principle." He compared the private interpretation of Scripture to the Babylonian Magi, " They retire as the sages of Babylon and make room for Daniel, the Church Catholic, the true prophet of God, who alone is able to give the dream and its interpretation." " The essence of revealed religion," he wrote, " is the submission of the reason to a positive system, the acquiescence in doctrine which cannot be proved or explained." He took for granted that there must be a promulgating authority, an infallible guide, somewhere, and because he failed to find it in the Church of England he turned to Rome. Frederick Temple, afterwards Archbishop of Canterbury, always insisted that this was Newman's great mistake. " Newman's great mistake was that he looked first for the true Church with the intention of believing what it taught, instead of looking for the truth and then adhering to the Church which taught it."[1] But most of the Tractarians held to a static view of Church authority, as though the Church had in its first days pronounced judgements on all the essential questions that could arise, and that it was possible to consult the mind of the early Church almost as one might consult an oracle.

"I believe," wrote Pusey, "our Lord's promise that the Holy Spirit should guide his Apostles into the whole truth and I believe that they faithfully and fully delivered the whole truth which they had received to those whom they appointed in their stead to carry on the lamp of truth to the end.   I cannot believe that the later Church is wiser than St. John the Divine.... In and through my mother the Church of England I became a disciple of the Fathers and believe all which they believed and reject all which they rejected."

The Tractarians were naïvely confident that there would be a general agreement as to what the voice of the early Church actually was, just as the Reformers believed that the Scriptures spoke with a voice as unmistakable as it was infallible.

" As to the question," wrote Keble to Pusey on November 26, 1850, " how do we know the

[1] See my *The Oxford Movement and After*.

mind of the undivided Church. I should have thought it was to be answered by each man for himself by the same kind of process as, e.g., a Roman Catholic knows the mind of his own present Church. It is a matter of fact, which he knows sometimes by reading, sometimes by consenting tradition. And the individual must use his own common sense." This was very well but under these conditions unanimity was impossible and the voice ceased to be oracular.

The word infallibility is unfortunate. It bears within it the sense of finality, of foreclosing the future, when all round us we have evidences of new knowledge undreamed of by our fathers. The word *indefectibility*,[1] as Professor N. P. Williams has pointed out, would be far better. Indefectibility means that while we believe that the Church will be so far guided that it will never lose essential truth, nevertheless it may from time to time arrive at mistaken conclusions, and harbour erroneous views. For instance, the Early Church universally believed that the second coming was to happen immediately. If no decision was arrived at the only reason was that no one questioned the belief. The very first General Council that ever met, in which Peter himself took

[1] In *Northern Catholicism.*

E

a leading part, and whose decisions he presumably accepted, decided that Christians were to abstain from " things strangled and from blood," that is, from animals which when slaughtered were not bled in the Jewish manner, a regulation which was soon treated as a dead letter. For centuries in the Western Church there was a practically unanimous belief in the eternity of a material hell-fire. For many centuries in the whole Church East and West the belief in verbal inspiration was pretty well universal. If there are no formal decisions affirming these beliefs it is because no one called them in question.

If we hold the doctrine of the indefectibility of the Church we must base it on a general conception of the Church, as the creation, or at least the re-creation of our Lord, and inspired by the Spirit, so that we feel it would be a failure of faith, a surrender to " defeatism," to think that the Church could make shipwreck concerning the faith. It is too precarious to base either infallibility, or indefectibility, on single texts, like " He shall guide you into all truth," or " The gates of hell shall not prevail against it." In neither case would there be any consensus of agreement on the part of scholars that we can be sure that we have our Lord's exact words, and they can at least be balanced by such a text as—" When the Son of Man comes shall He find faith upon the earth ? "

The Infallibility of Scripture.

If there is no infallible Person is there an infallible Book ? There has been in England as well as in America a revival of belief in the verbal inspiration of scripture, carrying with it the idea that in the Bible we have the Word of God, as dictated by the Holy Ghost, so that questions of authorship are unimportant. " What does it matter who holds the pen, if God is the writer ? " This belief has received the name of Fundamentalism. It corresponds to a common weakness of human nature, the desire for certainty. To some minds the conviction that the Bible is the Word of God gives the same sense of security, of feeling there is nothing further to worry about, as belief in the Infallibility of the Pope. " If you give that up " (the account of creation in Genesis as a literal statement of fact) a man said to me once, " you don't know where you are." " It's all or nothing," he added, " all or nothing." He felt that with the plenary authority of the Bible unimpaired, he was safe. But once begin to tamper with it, to say that in some passages there were mis-statements of fact ; that others were not meant to be taken literally ; that authors and dates were not what they seemed ; that the book of Daniel, for instance, was written long after the date of the fall of Babylon ; once admit these things and he would feel that the foundations of his faith were undermined and the whole edifice in danger of collapse.

This belief is shared by many people, and upheld with passionate enthusiasm. How did it originate ?

When the New Testament speaks of " the scriptures " it refers of course to the Old Testament, but though the Jew regarded the Old Testament as inspired no writer in the New Testament claimed that it was infallible. In the New Testament no book makes the claim of infallibility for itself with the possible exception of the Apocalypse. While the Church regarded books of the New Testament from the first as being inspired, since they were written by Apostles or inspired men, the view that they were verbally inspired, or infallible, is far from universal. " No one, I think, can doubt," wrote Origen, " that the statement that God walked in the afternoon in Paradise, and that Adam lay hid under a tree is related figuratively in Scripture,

that some mystical meaning may be attached to it."
Origen extended the same principle to the New
Testament. "And many other instances similar
to this (the Temptation) will be found in the
gospels by anyone who will read them with
attention and will observe that in the narratives
which appear to be literally recorded there are
inserted at intervals things which cannot be
admitted historically, but which may be accepted
in a spiritual meaning." Admittedly Origen
was unorthodox on some points but we have no
evidence that his views on inspiration were
considered unusual at Alexandria in his day. In
fact the Epistle of Barnabas, probably also
emanating from Alexandria, was regarded as
Scripture as late as the date of the Sinaitic Codex
(350 A.D.) and the Epistle of Barnabas is of the
same school of interpretation. Eusebius now
here suggests that Origen's views on Scripture
were unorthodox.

Bishop Gore has given other instances. "Thus
it was widely held that the opening chapters of
Genesis are allegorical and not historical—they
give us as St. Gregory of Nyssa said 'ideas (or
doctrines) in the form of a story.'" And Irenaeus,
who would be regarded as a literalist, is reported
by a later Greek writer who had more of his

text than remains to us, as having argued against the literal, and in favour of the allegorical, interpretation of the Fall.   And a fifth-century book *On the Catholic Faith*, ascribed to Boethius, gives us a general account of the divine revelation in Scripture as given us " under such a mode as is either the mode of history, which narrates only what happened, or the mode of allegory, which cannot represent the course of history, or a mode made up of those two so as to remain both historical and allegorical."   Again, St. Chrysostem when confronted with apparent discrepancies between the Evangelists, does not dispute their existence, but is content to plead that they showed the independence of the witnesses and do not touch the main points of the gospel.   Others held a similar view, and contended that some things in the epistles were not inspired, but simply human judgements.   Chrysostem boldly maintained that the ritual institution of the Old Testament law—" the sacrifices, and the purifications and the new moons and the ark and the temple itself—had their origin from Gentile grossness."

In the west belief in verbal inspiration became the rule.   There were two principal causes.   One was the influence of St. Augustine and Gregory

the Great, who were both literalists. The other
the barbarian invaders who in the fifth century
poured into the Roman Empire and devastated
Western Europe, and changed it from a civilized
state into the hunting grounds and spheres of
influence of warring barbarian tribes. The
ignorance and brutality which these invaders
brought into the Church made the doctrine of
verbal inspiration valuable and popular. The
Church needed before all else some authority
which would impress simple and savage minds.
It was a great thing to be able to reinforce the
authority of the Pope by appealing to an infallible
Bible. The Pope, in fact, found verbal inspiration a very useful weapon as he was able to support his pretensions by basing them on texts
like : " Thou art Peter," and " Feed My sheep."

Gregory the Great, who sent the other
Augustine to England in 597, did more than anyone else to fasten verbal inspiration round the
neck of the Church. He was a great man, a
popular and prolific writer, and his influence on
his own and future generations was enormous.
His views prevailed in the West for the next 500
years and were still powerful at the Reformation,
especially his views on inspiration, which he
expressed trenchantly, when he said in reply to

some question about the authorship of a book of the Bible. " What does it matter who held the pen if God is the writer ? " Gregory, indeed, was great as an administrator and a man of action, but, though reputed one of the Four Doctors of the Church, he was no great scholar or thinker. His ideas on inspiration still held sway when the Reformation began, and the Reformers while rejecting the authority of the Pope clung all the more tenaciously to the authority of the Bible. They exchanged, in fact, one infallibility for another, for though in a sense there had been two infallibilities, the infallible Pope and the infallible Word of God, yet in case of any disputed interpretation the Pope decided.

The leading Reformers had a naïve belief that if each individual interpreted the Bible by his private judgement, the Holy Ghost would lead all honest men to a harmonious result. Calvin worked out his theory of the authority of scripture in his Institutes. The Scriptures are the Word of God : nothing human is mixed up in them and their every affirmation is to be received with the deference which is due to the living voice of God speaking from heaven. " We are not favoured," he said in one place, " with daily

oracles from heaven " (meaning *viva voce* oracles),
" but to the divinely illuminated Christian oracles
are furnished by the Scripture." Here we get
the oracular theory of authority in so many words.

John Knox has left us an illuminating account
of his interview with Mary Queen of Scots, which
brings out the orthodox Protestant standpoint.
" You interpret the Scriptures," said she, " in
one manner, and they (the cardinals) in another ;
who will be judge ? " " Believe God," said he,
" that plainly speaketh in His Word ; and farther
than the word teacheth you, you shall neither
believe the one, nor the other ; the Word of
God is plain in itself ; and if there appear any
obscurity in one place, the Holy Ghost which
is never contradictious to Himself, explains the
same more clearly in other places ; so that there
can remain no doubt, but unto such as obstinately
will remain ignorant."

The view of the infallibility and oracular
authority of Scripture was generally held in
countries which had rejected the Pope except by
Anabaptists and their spiritual descendants, of
whom the Quakers are the best exemplars. These
held to the direct inspiration of the individual
by the Holy Ghost, independently of Scripture.
The Anabaptists contrasted the dead letter of

Scripture with the living voice of God in their hearts.

Until the last sixty or seventy years the inerrancy of Scripture was generally held. It is now generally abandoned, chiefly owing to two new developments of knowledge.

1. The theory of evolution as a principle of biological growth taught by Darwin in the *Origin of Species* published in 1859 has come to be generally accepted. This theory represents human life as having been gradually evolved from a lower to a higher state, instead of man being created at his highest *per saltum* and having since declined. It is impossible for those who accept this theory to regard the early chapters of Genesis as free from error.

2. The growth of knowledge not so much of the text of the Bible as in what is called the Higher Criticism, which takes into account language, contemporary beliefs, and the historical setting of the various books. Where for instance we find in the Book of Daniel words that only came into use many years after the conquests of Alexander the Great, i.e., after 333 B.C., it is difficult to believe that the author was a contemporary of *Darius* who captured Babylon two centuries earlier.

Highly as we value the scriptures for their teaching no English churchman need regard them as providing inspired oracles, nor every text as being verbally inspired. However much we may lament the loss of the infallible voice of scripture and feel that our parents' lot was cast in a world in which it was easier to believe than it is for most people to-day, still we are hiding our heads in the sand if we disregard the labours of scholars and the inescapable inferences dictated by our reason. The infallibility of the Bible, as of the Pope, is a bruised reed.

The conclusion, then, we have come to so far is that infallibility, that is an infallible voice proceeding from the Church, whether from Pope, Council, or Scripture, is a delusion. There is no such thing. But while rejecting this conception we may still hold that the Spirit guides the Church, that it will not abandon essential truth, and that it rightly teaches with authority, though that authority is not infallible, nor even oracular in the sense that it is impious to question its teaching.

Authority not Oracular.

But though we may reject the idea of infallibility, that is the belief that any person, or set of

people, or any book, has laid down, or can lay
down, judgements on religion, or morals, that
are final, inerrant, and irreformable, or even an
Oracular Authority that must be received with
submission, and in silence even if we disagree
with it, this is not to deny the need of authority
in religion.

Our Roman and Fundamentalist friends have
troubled the waters by insisting that this authority
must be infallible, or at least oracular. But why
should there not be an authority to which we
attach great weight, whose decisions we respect
and to which we defer, but which we reserve to
ourselves the right of questioning? In the field
of natural science the great ones, like Galileo,
Copernicus, Newton, or Darwin, still exercise
authority but not oracular authority.

A man decides to set out to seek a far country.
Books have been written about it and maps
published. Travellers profess to have made the
journey, or part of it. Still a good deal of
mystery surrounds it. Many of the tales concerning it are admittedly travellers' tales. They
are far from being infallible. Nevertheless he
would be a fool if he decided he could learn
nothing from them and, because some of the
directions given him were misleading, to assume

that he could do without any directions at all, still less that the country he is seeking has no existence. To reject the infallibility of dogmatic decisions is not to deny that they may, and indeed should, carry great weight, nor even that they express, though imperfectly on account of the imperfection of language, absolute truth.

The Bishop of Bangor recently contrasted sacred and profane truth. If he is reported correctly he stated that while no profane " truth " could be regarded as final, being at any moment liable to be supplanted, or modified, sacred " truth " was something determined beyond doubt. This seems rather crudely put, at any rate as reported. I imagine that the most revolution-ary-minded astronomers believe it to be an absolute truth that the earth goes round the sun. On the other hand I should maintain that there are religious truths, such as the Incarnation, which are in a sense absolute, that is not liable to be abandoned or superseded—but I submit. (1) That in theory there is no inherent reason why language expressing those truths should not from time to time be modified, and (2) that these truths are open to the fullest examination by the faithful as well as the outsider.

In the last resort if we have to deal with an

unsettled, inquiring seeker after truth, whether a member of the Church, or an outsider, we ask him to believe not because the Church, or the Bible, tells him, but because when he has examined all the evidence as far as he can, we hope that the religion which we present to him will appeal to his sense of truth, his conviction of what is right, and his feeling for beauty.

The *raison d'être* of the Church is the possession of the knowledge of God but we have no right to suppose that this knowledge has come down to us crystal clear, without mist or incrustation. The Church is our God given guide; it has a claim on our respectful consideration. If on any great question we reject its judgement we can do so only with reluctance and hesitation.

Where and how then is the authority of the Church expressed?

(1) *In Holy Scripture.*

The most important source of Church authority is Holy Scripture, because it is the only source from which we derive first-hand knowledge of our Lord's life and teaching, of the life and teaching of the Apostles, and of the history of the infant Church from the Resurrection down to about A.D. 90. It is reasonably certain that for the teaching of Christianity before A.D. 90 we know nothing outside the pages of the New Testament. The Old Testament also contains authoritative teaching of great importance but it lies somewhat outside the scope of this book.

What authority, then, do we allow to Scripture? Certainly not an infallible authority. The Puritans wished to make Scripture the sole authority whether for faith, conduct, or worship. Hooker in his controversy with Thomas Cartwright contested the position that nothing was to be allowed in the ceremonial of the Church for which a positive injunction of Holy Scripture could not be found. The Church of England definitely rejected this contention by laying down that " A National Church hath power to ordain Rites and Ceremonies."

The authority the Articles gave to Scripture was negative. They enjoined only that nothing was to be insisted on as necessary to salvation which is not " read therein nor may be proved thereby." This is a principle of great importance. It may be objected that it hinders the free development of the Church and favours a static and unprogressive form of religion. But human nature being what it is, we have to remember that a religion may change for the worse as well as for the better. If we compare the teaching of Zarathrustra, or Buddha or Mohammed, with popular Zoroastrianism, Buddhism or Islam, we shall see how each, in turn, has deteriorated. It has been the great strength of Christianity that it has treasured records of its Founder and His disciples, which give us a kind of authentic bed-rock of His teaching, to which all bodies of Christians profess allegiance.

The advocate of unfettered development might say : " I admit this. I do not reject a word of the New Testament. All I claim is that there may be essential doctrines which were at first hidden, which are not explicit in the New Testa-ment, but have since been authenticated by the Church and are now articles of faith, and no longer merely pious opinions."

The difficulty seems to be to know when to stop. Belief in the Immaculate Conception of our Lady has been an article of faith necessary to salvation for Roman Catholics since 1854. There is not a word about it in the New Testa-ment. It may be said to be an inference, not from Scripture, but from the unscriptural teaching and devotional practices which had become prevalent in the Middle Ages. It was an inference which devout Catholics for centuries refused to accept—

the great Dominican Order, indeed, argued against it for generations. Yet this belief by the *fiat* of the Pope is now necessary for salvation.

There is a danger, perhaps, of being too static, of holding fast to antiquity and becoming petrified. That danger may have been real in the early days of the Tractarians, but in a changing world where the watchword is progress, it is not a danger that besets us now. Popularity is a poor test of truth. We may defend non-scriptural beliefs and practices as for example the invocation of saints ; we may try to persuade others to adopt them. Any particular church may adopt them as part of its own economy. The Church of England only lays down the general principle that no belief or practice is to be insisted on as necessary to salvation unless it has scriptural authority.

As to the interpretation of Scripture there are mercifully certain self-evident facts, concerning the life and teaching of our Lord, about which there is pretty general agreement. On disputed points of exegesis there is no oracle we can consult. It was natural for the Tractarians in their reverence for Church authority and their distrust of Liberalism to assume that there was an authorized *Church* interpretation of disputed passages. But the case, in reality, is not so simple. The labour of scholars is progressive. Their work goes on. Texts that the Church has accepted as genuine are first rejected by a small minority of scholars, then by the general body of intelligent people who know something about the subject. It is a long time before the text is officially repudiated. The famous text of St. John v, 7, about the Three Heavenly Witnesses was rejected by Erasmus in the sixteenth century, and by Richard Simon in 1689. Porson the English scholar, gave it its *coup de grâce* in 1790. Our Revisers omitted it in 1881 but as late as 1897 the Holy Office forbade it to be called in question. It was not until 1905 that it was given up by Rome.

Knowledge based, not on guesses, but on scientific inquiry gets established and, in time, permeates. It is far better that there should be no official interpretation or judgement. It will always be behind the times. Those who are sufficiently interested to take some trouble can find out what at any given moment is the consensus of expert opinion as to the genuineness or the interpretation of any disputed text. But there is no oracular or infallible voice.

AUTHORITY 67

(2) *Tradition.*

By Tradition we mean that deposit of faith, morals, and ceremonial, of things to be believed and practised as part of the custom or tradition of the Church. The oldest part of Tradition is, indeed, Scripture. The Tradition of the Church was in existence so that St. Paul could appeal to it before the New Testament was written. It was Tradition which guaranteed the sacredness of Scripture, which has come down to us unauthenticated by Pope or Council, and was recognized as sacred on the authority of Tradition by which, and by which alone, Christians learnt which of the early Christian writings were to be regarded as Scripture and which not.[1]

We find Tradition embodied in the creeds, in writings of the Fathers, codified in the decrees of Councils so far as they have been accepted by the Church and have not fallen into desuetude;

[1] It is remarkable that this question of which books preserved by the Church were to be considered as possessing a special sanctity was never, at least before the Council of Trent, the subject of a formal conciliar decision. The issue " was the result of a common life and not of any formal action. There is not the slightest evidence to show that the collection of the sacred-books, as the depositaries of doctrine, was ever the subject of a conference of the Churches. The Bible was formed, even as the Church was formed, by the action of that Holy Spirit which is the life of both."

Westcott. *The Bible in the Church*, p. 293.

it is included in the elastic word *custom*. " If any man seems to be contentious," said St. Paul, " we have no such custom neither the Churches of God."[1]

To ignore all this, to treat the history of the Church as of no account, to act as if you could begin *de novo* with the Reformation, or John Wesley, or the Group Movement, is to treat a living organism as if it were a dead body, or a piece of machinery. Charles Marriott, a disciple of Newman, and one of the saints of the movement who neither lost his head nor heart when the crash came in 1845, wrote : " I shall rather maintain that there is a truly divine tradition in the Church . . . which is represented with tolerable fairness by the consenting testimony of various students. It is upon such a tradition (collected as I believe with supernatural aid) that the decrees of councils are framed." Nevertheless, though he thought such a Tradition a real source of truth he did not claim infallibility for it. " I take the position," he added, " of submitting all to a future general Council and holding my view of disputed points as an opinion."

It is important to remember that Tradition is not only concerned with the past. It is the past

[1] 1 Cor. xi, 16.

living on into the present. It is above all living and not dead. Indeed it is the business of the Church to slough off the dead past not as a whole like a snake, but bit by bit as does the living human body its outworn tissues. The Church like any other organism, can no more live on its past than it can cut itself adrift from it. The Tractarians in their rejection of Rome with its non-Scriptural beliefs and practices and the reaction from Evangelicalism and Liberalism, which were contemptuous of tradition, leant too much to antiquity. It seemed clear to Pusey that the Apostles knew more than we did and the Golden Age of the Church, as of mankind, was in the past, and every change for the worse. " Back to the Apostles and the primitive Church " therefore was the Tractarian cry. J. A. Froude called himself and his friends " Apostolicals." It was a cry which might have resulted in sterile antiquarianism, yet looking back on the history of the last century sterility is the last word we should apply to Tractarianism. It must be said in extenuation that the theory of evolution, which is by us taken for granted, was to them unknown. That mankind was continually developing and for the most part for the better, was to them unthinkable.

Newman, before he left us, to justify his action propounded the theory of development in theology to account for prevalent beliefs and practices in the Roman Church for which he could find no warrant in Scripture. Put very crudely the theory is that as the acorn develops into the oak, and the mountain stream into a mighty river, so the Church, being a living organism, develops and produces features, of which not much more than the embryos were present in its infancy. I have maintained that it would not be possible to discover even the embryo of, for instance, papal Infallibility in Scripture; still, we must recognize that Newman, with the insight of a man of genius, discovered in development an indispensable principle of the life of the Church. The Church develops because it lives and grows. The Orthodox Church of the East, conservative and rooted in the most ancient customs and traditions as it is, does yet preserve the principle of development by its insistence that Tradition is not merely the opinion of antiquity, but the sentiment and the unexpressed as well as the expressed judgements of the living Church.

We repudiate Roman developments not because they are developments, but because that is just what they are not. That is if we regard the

Church of the New Testament as the embryo
they are inconsistent with it. They are new and
illegitimate births. They are monstrous accre-
tions on the original stock. They are sports.
Now the Church of England certainly allows the
principle of development. It is not content to
lay down that the faith or use of the first two
or four or six or ten centuries is sufficient for all
time. Development is a fact. If we consider
the enormous change in the faith of the Church of
England that has taken place in the last century
on such all important questions as the nature of
scriptural inspiration and the state of the lost, or
the extraordinary developments in worship, we
can hardly doubt this.

The late Marquis of Salisbury was once walking
with two English Bishops when one of them used
the phrase : " The mind of the Church of England." " You interest me amazingly," Lord
Salisbury is reported to have said, " I didn't know
the Church of England had a mind." There is
some ground for this gibe but nevertheless it
is a fact the Church of England has a mind, but it
is slow to make it up. It is the opposite of cock-
sure. It is inclined to think that the minority
may have something to say for itself. It is very
cautious and believes that the wisest solutions

are the result of the slow working out of difficulties in practice, of much argument and discussion and the clash of mind with mind. We are sometimes taunted with this apparent indecision as being weak, feeble, vacillating, and characteristic of the Church of England. The taunt may be borne in patience. The alternative seems to be to make decisive pronouncements, which no one is allowed to contradict but which may be untrue, and are eventually discarded. On what subject is a definite decision more needed than on the Bible? Yet in face of the clearest evidence the Roman Catholic is told to believe that Matthew was written before Mark and that there are no errors in Holy Scripture.

The Orthodox Church is, surely, right when, while maintaining its belief in a living tradition, it is much more chary of giving this tradition definite expression. The Church of England believes in the working of the Holy Spirit in the Church, but it realizes that He works through men, and that it is a slow process before their pride, stubbornness, and stupidity, will admit the light, and that even when the light shines in the heart it can only find expression through the lips and pens of fallible men. The Roman Church while believing in the power of the Holy

Spirit believes also in the power of fallible man to pronounce infallible judgements. If we think of the decisions the Church of England might have been committed to during the past century on Biblical criticism, and on the nature of eternal punishment, we may well feel that its deliberate slowness in deciding, and its apparent inarticulateness are points for which we have no reason to be ashamed. What seems cowardice is in reality waiting on God.

CHAPTER III

TRADITION APPLIED

" If we have to submit as I think we must to an imperfect rationalization of belief, this ought not to be because in a fit of intellectual despair we are driven to treat reason as a delusion, but because reason itself assures us that such a course is, at the lowest, the least irrational one open to us.   If we have to find our way over difficult seas and under murky skies without compass or chronometer, we need not on that account allow the ship to drive at random.   Rather ought we to weigh with the more anxious care every indication, be it positive or negative, and from whatever quarter it may come, which can help us to guess our position and to lay the course which it behoves us to steer."

LORD BALFOUR, *Foundations of Belief*, p. 234.

" Authority does not cease to be authority because it is not final and absolute."

STAUNTON, *Place of Authority in Religious Belief*.

IF we wish to understand the place of tradition in the system of the *Via Media*, it is necessary to see how it works in actual practice.   This can best be considered under four heads : Faith, Sacraments, Worship and Holy Orders.

1. FAITH

With regard to Faith the Church of England accepts the three Creeds, and though the Athanasian symbol is to-day partly shelved, not on account of the faith which it expresses, but because of the anathemas with which it is involved, the authority of the other two is insisted on.

The thirty-nine Articles of Religion, to which the assent of the clergy of the Church of England is required, have been a great bugbear in the eyes of those members of the Eastern Church who examined them in the eighteenth and nineteenth centuries. They need not have been. They were articles of peace and designed to make the *Via Media* of the English Church as wide as possible. On the surface they make a decidedly Protestant impression. It was a common saying at one time that the Prayer Book was Catholic but the Articles Protestant. But Newman in Tract XC, though it drew upon his devoted head so much vituperation that he felt he had no longer a place in the Church of England, was able to show that the condemnations in the articles were not so much of official Catholic doctrine as of popular Roman teaching, and that they could bear a Catholic interpretation.

Such as they are the Articles lost very much of

their force when the original form of Assent was given up, which ran :

" I, A.B. do willingly and from my heart subscribe to the Thirty-nine Articles of Religion and to the three articles in the Thirty-sixth Canon, and to all things therein contained."

The Declaration substituted in 1871 is as follows :

" I assent to the thirty-nine Articles of Religion and to the Book of Common Prayer, and of Ordering of Bishops, Priests, and Deacons. I believe the doctrine of the Church of England as therein set forth to be agreeable to the Word of God." It is a general assent to the articles as a whole, not a specific assent to every statement they contain.

The articles are not binding on the laity, and are to be considered as the peculiar property of the Church of England rather than a possession of the *Via Media*.

The Creeds are on an altogether different footing. In the Church of England the Apostles' Creed is recited daily, at Morning and Evening Prayer. It is repeated clause by clause in an interrogatory form to the Godparents at every Infant Baptism, requiring the answer " All this I steadfastly believe." The Nicene Creed is recited at every Eucharist. Further, belief in some articles of the Creeds is reaffirmed in the Proper Prefaces which are a part of that service. Thus in the Proper Preface for Christmas the celebrant affirms that Jesus Christ, " by the operation of the Holy Ghost, was made very man of the substance of the Virgin Mary his mother." In that for Ascension, that Jesus Christ, " after his most glorious Resurrection manifestly appeared to all his Apostles and in their sight ascended up into heaven."

There is to-day, and has been for many years, a strong objection to creeds in certain quarters. " A creed," says Professor Kirsopp Lake, " is the petrifaction of opinion." He means presumably that when a creed is drawn up it takes on the colour of current ideas in philosophy which remain embedded in it when the ideas are obsolete. It is of course true that there are fashions in philosophy as in other things and there is a danger that the creed may be inextricably involved, not only with fundamental truths, but with temporary philosophical fashions. " Had a new formula," says Dr. Sorley, " been produced in England twenty or thirty years it is safe to say it would have been an amalgam of the ideas of Hegel and Darwin." Even if that statement be true, though a very good argument against re-writing the creeds to-day, it is not necessarily a valid objection to creeds drawn up centuries ago. It is unreasonable to say that there is no such thing as permanent and absolute religious truth or that it can only be expressed in a form that will cease to be true for future generations. One only has to go through the Apostles Creed, article by article, to see how little philosophy has to do with it.

Some form of creed is necessary if the Church is to exist. A creed implies a basis of intellectual agreement about God and the world. There can be no fellowship in Church life and worship between those who believe in God and those who do not, between those who believe that Jesus Christ is God and those who believe He was only a man, however gifted : between those who believe in the continual presence and guidance of a personal Spirit, and those who admit only an impersonal influence. There must be some common measure of agreement on these points. Whether an objective standard in faith be a spiritual necessity or not, it is a psychological and practical necessity.

The theologians who drew up our Nicene Creed were face to face with those who denied that God created the world, that Jesus was really and truly God, and also really and truly man, and that the Holy Ghost had a personal and individual existence in the Godhead. It is possible that its phraseology might be improved for modern minds. It is certain that by the time the present modernists had got it altered to their liking it would be out of date for the generation that would have arisen. No human words can be adequate to define the nature and being of God. At best a creed is a rough summary of the fundamentals of Christianity, which can only be an approximate expression of divine truth. Those who clamour for a re-statement of the faith and demand that the creeds should be re-written seem to me to under-rate the difficulty of the task. Producing fresh creeds for each generation must always be a desperate undertaking, as the creed writers will always be a generation behind. It would certainly take at least twenty years to get a creed accepted, by which time it would no longer be " modern " to the generation just grown up.

It is worth remarking that the commonest objections to creeds are not so much to matters of opinion concerning the nature and being of God, as for example " being of our substance with the Father," as to matters of fact with regard

to certain historical events alleged in the Creed to
have occurred in the earthly life of Jesus Christ,
though, of course, these events have theological
implications. No one, for instance, who
accepts the Virgin Birth will question that our
Lord was really and truly God. Whether these
historical events did happen may be a question
for debate. But no change in philosophic
opinion since the creeds were drawn up has
made it more or less credible whether our Lord's
miraculous birth, His death, and His bodily
Resurrection, actually happened. To belief
in these events all the Churches of the *Via
Media* are committed. Attempts have been
been made in the Church of England to allow the
admission of clergy who reject them, but the
affirmation of the Upper House of the Convocation of Canterbury in 1905 still holds good :
" That this House is resolved to maintain unimpaired the Catholic Faith, in the Holy Trinity
and the Incarnation, as contained in the Apostles'
and Nicene Creeds and the Quicunque Vult,
and regards the faith then presented, both in
statements of doctrine and statements of fact, as
the necessary basis on which the teaching of the
Church reposes."

I also notice that many of those who dislike

what Professor Lake calls "petrifaction" in theology do not object to fixed dogmatic statements in morals. But the moderns who reject the Christian faith are for the most part equally hostile to Christian morals. If it is petrifying to be content to believe, as the early Christians believed, that Jesus was very God of very God, it is just as petrifying to hold that love, self-denial, and sexual purity are permanent elements in the ideal character.

2. SACRAMENTS

The Sacraments, both Baptism and Holy Communion, and the five rites, "commonly called sacraments," Confirmation, Holy Orders, Matrimony, Penance, Unction, form another and a very important part of tradition.

The Sacraments may be defined loosely as certain guaranteed ways in which man is brought into touch with the divine through some external visible means. Men used to look on matter and spirit as being divided into watertight compartments. The tendency of modern science has been to regard them as more and more closely intertwined. They act and react on one another. In a very real sense all material life is sacramental. A sunset, a picture, a chord of music, the touch of a hand, a voice, the scent of a flower, all alike may bring to us power and illumination from God. In the Sacraments we have trysting places in which we believe we have a guarantee that God will meet us.

It is certain that the need for sacraments was never greater than it is to-day. The world is so much with us, and our minds so occupied with the pleasures, business, and cares of daily life, that God is too often shut out, not wilfully, but through our preoccupation with other things. Christ knocks at the door and we don't open because we are too busy to hear. The modern world is not aware of God. Boswell records of Dr. Johnson that once meeting an old school-friend whom he had not seen since they were boys together, he asked him what he had done with his life and received the surprising reply: " I have tried to be a philosopher but somehow cheerfulness will keep breaking in." Sacraments are definite ways in which God breaks in, and in which man by faith can lay hold of God. On the whole, and allowing that there are other causes at work, it is probably true to say that Catholics who have valued Sacraments, are more aware of God than Protestants, who have, on the whole, neglected them.

It is interesting to note that Dr. Lake, for many years a leading exponent of Modernism, in his book *The Religion of Yesterday and To-morrow*, called attention to what he considers three failures of Protestantism. Two of them have to do with the comparative disuse of Sacraments. " Protestantism," he says, " has failed to supply adequately the need of sacraments which are a permanent element in Catholicism, which Protestants have never been able fully to assimilate." The importance of sacraments in his eyes is that they form points of contact with the unseen world. He thinks that for the uneducated, " the Mass affords an insight into the mystical value of life, lit up by the splendour of divine grace."

Twenty-five years ago an American Protestant, Dr. Newman Smyth, in a book entitled *Passing Protestantism and Coming Catholicism* ascribed the failure of Protestant worship in America to attract and hold the coming generation to its non-sacramental character. The sense of this poverty in Protestant worship has found eloquent expression in the writings of two Nonconformists, Mr. Orchard and Mr. Peck. " The whole idea of worship," wrote Mr. Orchard while still a Nonconformist, " suffers from its non-sacramental character. The worship of the Protestant

Churches is failing to satisfy aesthetic demands, psychological conditions, and religious feeling, and is gradually being deserted." That " the central and most prominent part of worship ought to be the Holy Communion," was Mr. W. G. Peck's thesis, before he joined the Church of England and, while yet a Nonconformist, he wrote a book—*The Value of the Sacrament* to prove and illustrate his point.

The third failure of Protestantism, according to Dr. Lake, is its failure to provide skilled assistance in ministration to the spiritually sick, as is done by Catholics in the sacrament of penance. Dr. Lake is contemptuous of prayers for the sick body, but it is becoming more and more widely recognized that there is a ministry of healing for body as well as soul, for which the Church made provision in the sacrament of Unction, which was omitted from the Prayer Book in 1552 and has not yet been restored, though there is a movement on foot for its revival, and its use is increasing. With regard to ministration to the sick soul, provision is made in the Prayer Book for confession and a form of absolution is provided.

Finally, it may be said that the Churches of the *Via Media* have held fast to the traditional belief that sacraments are not bare signs, and only operative because they rouse faith in the recipient but have a real objective value as channels and means of conveying divine grace.   At the same time, as regards the Eucharist, the Church of England, at least, while holding to the reality of the mystical presence of Christ's Body and Blood, has refused to define its nature.

3. WORSHIP

There is no point on which the difference between Catholic and Protestant is more felt than in their respective conceptions of worship.   The one is mainly received from tradition, the other aspires to be the free expression of the mind of the worshipper.   One looks at it chiefly as an opportunity for giving, the other as a means of receiving.   One regards the edification it bestows as the result of the subconscious effect of the service as a whole : the other as the direct appeal of the minister to the heart and mind of the worshipper.   The one feels he has been rewarded if he goes away feeling that he has been in the presence of God ; the other if he feels that he has heard something which he thinks has done him good.   It is in the sphere of worship that the Church of the *Via Media* has its hardest task, since some of its members are inclined to one extreme ; some to the other.

" Worship," says Mr. Brabant, " is the joyous abasement of our whole selves before the Divine Mystery as the source and sustainer of our lives " ; and we may accept the definition as approximately true. The worshipper is moved by wonder and awe, culminating in praise. This sense of awe lies at the heart of all true worship, as Professor Otto has reminded us.

There are two sides to worship. There is what Mr. Brabant calls the *expressive side*. The worshipper tries to express his wonder and praise. There is also the *impressive* side. The worshipper receives within himself some sense of the Mystery of God, and is helped or edified in various ways. A writer in the *Church Times* recently stated that the sole object of the worshippers should be to give. He should expect to get nothing. But this is a mistake. The devout person of robust faith and a sanguine temperament may think he needs only to express his feelings of enthusiastic love and praise, but he deceives himself. He is all the time receiving in his worship aids to his faith, though he may not be aware of it. If his sun were darkened and God withdrew the sense of His Presence he would very quickly feel the need

of receiving. Like the Psalmist his cry would be—
"Out of the deep have I called unto Thee: O
Lord hear my voice."

Our first motive may be, perhaps should be, to
render thanks and praise, but we also hope to
receive. The best gift we can receive is a realiza-
tion of the Divine Mystery; to be able to say—
"Surely God is in this place." But we may also
hope to have faith strengthened, our knowledge
of God deepened, our petitions heard, and our
whole self made more ready to face the problems
and difficulties, spiritual, moral and intellectual,
of every-day life.

The mechanism of worship consists of words,
together with appropriate action accompanying
the words, or ceremonial; it includes dress and
ornaments, music very often, and an architectural
setting nearly always.

The mediæval tradition had been to disparage
words by reciting them, often inaudibly, and
always in an unknown tongue. The Protestant
in a fervour of reaction disparaged everything
except the words. The Church of England broke
with mediæval tradition in two ways, first by
returning to the primitive custom of using the
vernacular instead of Latin, saying the services
audibly, and inviting all to take part not only with

the heart but with the understanding, and secondly, by providing for lay people services other than the Mass.

We may well ask what causes brought about the practice of inaudibility which at first sight seems so strange and irrational and was apparently forbidden in advance by St. Paul? The reason given—at least for inaudibility in the Mass—by Dr. Harris is that the use of muttering, or the *vox mystica*,[1] as it came to be called, was meant to convey to the worshipper a sense of mystery. It seems more likely that the clinging to a language which only became dead by degrees, was a piece of conservatism, while inaudibility was the natural result of the service being said in a language not understood by the congregation. A strange tongue and inaudibility go hand in hand. In the West, Latin, the language of the Mass, had ceased to be the vulgar tongue certainly since the sixth century by which time hordes of Goths and Germans had poured into the Church. Inaudibility was not officially prescribed until the eighth century. From that date it was the rule.

It was therefore in the sixteenth century a great

---

[1] A Russian scholar, Father Florovsky, has suggested that the *vox mystica* originally meant a particular intonation and had nothing to do with inaudibility.

break with mediæval tradition to have all services, including the Mass, both in English, and audible.

As regards its expressive side, worship, by a congregation which cannot hear or understand, is only very imperfectly a corporate act. Each member of it may be engaged in devotion, but it is private not corporate devotion, if there is no common prayer in which all may join. When Cyril the Apostle of the Slavs was rebuked by the Pope and the rulers of the Church at Rome for having Mass sung in the Slavonic tongue, he snatched up a Psalter and read : " Omnis spiritus laudet Dominum." " Let everything that hath breath praise the Lord," saying, " If everything that hath breath is to praise the Lord, why my fathers do you forbid us to perform the Mass in the Slavonic tongue, or to translate other things from Latin and Greek into the vernacular ? " We are told that his arguments were successful and he was permitted to continue the use of the vernacular. " How shall he that filleth the place of the unlearned," wrote St. Paul to the Corinthians, " say Amen at the giving of thanks, seeing he knoweth not what thou sayest ? "

Now no one wants a congregation at Mass to be like a racing eight—absolutely " together," all doing the same thing at exactly the same time, but having the service audible and in the vernacular alone make possible a *corporate* expression of worship. It is always possible for individuals to turn a deaf ear to the service and engage in private devotions, if they wish, but all the time the main stream of intelligible worship goes on, which the individual rivulets can rejoin when they like. As for being distracted, many people find an audible recitation of prayer less distracting than an unintelligible muttering. Silence of course is most valuable, but silence and inaudibility are different things.

The *Via Media* can point to one Roman Catholic of unimpeachable orthodoxy as a witness in favour of audibility, namely, the late Pope Pius X, who declared that " active participation in the public and solemn prayer of the church is the primary and indispensable source of a true Christian spirit," and urged the faithful " to pray the mass not to pray at the mass."

On the impressive and receptive side the objections to unintelligibility are also considerable. It infects some minds, we understand, with awe and a sense of mystery, but not all. In fact, no excuse is more commonly given even by laymen with definitely Catholic sympathies for non-attendance at Anglo-Catholic churches than—" I cannot hear what is said." But it would require very much more cogent reasons than we ever hear given to justify a practice on the face of it so unreasonable.[1] "We approach the Altar," writes Mr. Brabant, "with our definite petitions, our orderly liturgy, our meditations on scripture, even our reasoned discourses and sermons. We offer up the whole of our personality, and the fire descends on our offering. There is in worship (I speak, of course, of ideal worship) the negative moment—what Otto calls the sense of the Numinous. Our words quiver into silence ; our thoughts lose themselves in infinity, our feelings tremble before the formless ; our righteousness becomes uncleanness. Before the Greatness of God we are nothing." This is finely said, but audibility and intelligibility should help, not hinder, such a consummation.

Outside the Mass in the occasional offices of the church, in the Baptism, Wedding and Funeral rites, unintelligibility is even more irrational. It is difficult to see how anyone can be more suitably impressed at a funeral, wedding or christening, with a due sense of the Divine Mystery if he is unable to understand what is said, than if the words are intelligible.

[1] The late Lord Halifax whom no one could accuse of any leaning towards Protestantism had a strong dislike to inaudibility in the Mass.

The practice has been revived and is spreading in the Church of England, and like the sand in the Sahara and in parts of Australia is threatening to turn once fertile land into a desert. Those who in this way wish to go behind the Reformation in thus disparaging the need of intelligibility in public prayer and consequently its value as a corporate act, may find some support in the non-episcopal churches. At least Mr. E. R. Micklem after asking the rhetorical question—" How should prayers be conducted so that they may be most easily followed by the inevitably slow moving mind of the congregation? " appends the following comment in a note. " For great sections of the Church, of course, this is an unnecessary question. It is not intended, they would say, that the prayers uttered by the minister should be followed in detail by the congregation. The present chapter assumes however that the ideal of Free Church worship is common prayer."[1]

The Russian Church is more successful, perhaps, than either the Church of Rome or the Church of England, in conveying a sense of the presence of God, at any rate as it impresses one ignorant of Russian. Though the priest is for considerable periods unseen and unheard, the

[1] *Christian Worship*, p. 195.

deacon and choir and congregation carry on by themselves audibly, with occasional irruptions from behind the screen, when the priest is seen and heard, seeming to suggest the breaking through of the Divine into the world of sense.

The other great departure from tradition in the Prayer Book was the provision of services for lay folk outside the Mass. Two motives were at work. One was positive: to make the Psalms and Scripture part of the devotional life of lay people. The only service that lay people were in the habit of attending was the Mass, in which there was very little scripture and no Psalms. This concentration on the Mass was not, however, primitive. The Church had taken over from the Jews the custom of making the recitation of the Psalms the core of worship, that is outside the Mass, and the service of the Hours, contained in the Breviary, consisted very largely of Psalms. To the Breviary, however, there were three outstanding objections. (1) Its services were only recited by priests and religious. (2) Even those who used them recited only a few comparatively of the Psalms. (3) The difficulty of the complicated rules for adjusting the services to the varying dates of Easter was so great that it took as long to find what was to be said as to say it when found. On the Continent an attempt to meet this last difficulty was made by Cardinal de Quinones who compiled a Reformed Breviary. Over here services in English which lay people could use were provided in the Bishops Book of 1537, supplemented by the Litany in English published in 1544. The provision therefore in Mattins and Evensong in 1549, of services for the laity in which the whole psalter was recited during the month, and which included lessons from scripture, forming no small a part of the service, was both a return to primitive use and a development of a tendency which was already making itself felt.

Another motive for providing Mattins, at least, was the dislike of solitary Masses felt by the Reformers. The officiant was forbidden to celebrate unless there were at least three communicants besides himself, intending communicants being required to give in their names beforehand. Should the requisite number of communicants not be forthcoming the officiant is directed to conclude the service after the Prayer for the Church Militant with a Collect and the Blessing. There is here obviously a good deal left to the discretion of the individual parish priest. He may recite Mattins and the ante-Communion service, and then conclude; or, provided he has three communicants, he may complete the Eucharist; in either case he appears to have obeyed the law. It may be presumed that the Henrician priests for the most part continued to celebrate, instead of breaking off with the Prayer for the Church Militant, but as they died out and were succeeded by men ordained when Protestantism was in the ascendant the celebration became the exception instead of the rule.

One of the most striking effects of the Oxford Movement has been the revival of the sung Eucharist and its substitution for Mattins on Sunday morning. The absence of clear and definite directions has, indeed, brought about a great practical difficulty in the worship of the Church of England, namely, the question of the Sung Eucharist as an alternative to Mattins on Sunday morning. Those on the Catholic side of the centre prefer a sung Eucharist, the more Protestant-minded, Mattins. Some churches manage to provide both. Here the *Via Media* is at a disadvantage. It is untidy. People don't always know what service they will get. But there are compensations. There is much to be said for the sung Eucharist. The sense of mystery it conveys is greater; the space for private prayer more ample ; the devotional atmosphere warmer ; the presence of God more easily realized. It is in the line of Church tradition.

Nevertheless those who prefer Mattins have a right to exist. Many of them have already made their Communion at an earlier celebration, and even devout Roman Catholics do not make a practice of assisting at *two* Masses in one day. There are many who dislike a sung Eucharist, it may be through prejudice, or that its devotional temperature is too warm for their constitutions, or that they revolt against the sense of mystery which transcends their capacity to realize. The loss may be theirs but it seems better to give such people a service that appeals to them, than to lose them altogether. Mattins does after all provide a way in which the worshipper can express his feelings of devotion, and through the Psalms and prayers, music, and ceremonial, can not only be edified but catch something of the mystery of God.

On these two points, then, the Prayer Book made definite breaks with mediæval tradition, though each represents, the one wholly, the other partly, a return to primitive practice. In other respects it was on the whole faithful to mediæval tradition. The Protestant cry when the Prayer

Book was drawn up was for a clean break with the past, which meant abandoning the traditional prayers, ceremonial, music, vestments and ornaments. In his zeal the Protestant tried to do away with the aesthetic appeal, whether to eye or ear, altogether. Churches were stripped, stained-glass windows destroyed, organs removed. The ideal was a plainly-clad minister, preaching and praying in a perfectly bare and barn-like church. Since the Reformation Protestants have completely changed their views about the appeal to the ear, and they use music freely. Their views on architecture have also enlarged, but except in the case of a few eccentrics, they do not seek to create an effect by presenting worship as a spectacle.

Catholic worship on the other hand relies on producing its effect largely through a spectacular display. Its appeal is on the surface less rational. The impression reaches the heart through the eye, though music is often called in to assist with its appeal to the ear. When ceremonial was revived in the Church of England a favourite word of abuse by those who disliked it was *theatrical*. In a sense all ceremonial is theatrical, because it makes its effect through the eye. As Mr. Brabant points out, the sting lies in the

H

suggestion of insincerity. If we call it dramatic it is another matter. Protestant worship by disdaining ceremonial has to create its effect largely by sermons, the singing of hymns, and *ex tempore* prayers. He has to improve every occasion with suitable words. It does not let the service speak for itself.

Having once broken with Rome the English reformers would have found their task easier if they had followed on Protestant lines and so obtained the enthusiastic support of Geneva, as Knox did in Scotland. Nevertheless in spite of advice from Zurich, Geneva, and Edinburgh, they held to the middle path. A sermon to be preached at least every Sunday and Holy Day to make the service edifying. On the other hand, on the aesthetic side the Ornaments Rubric was retained, which prescribed : " The Chancels shall remain as they have done in times past. And here it is to be noted, that such Ornaments of the Church and of the Minister thereof, at all times of their ministration, shall be retained and be in use, as were in this Church of England by the authority of Parliament, in the Second Year of the Reign of King Edward the Sixth."

The Prayer Book, it is true, contains very few directions on ceremonial for the simple reason

that the 1559 book was put into the hands of
priests who were familiar with the traditional
ceremonial, and, therefore, unless otherwise
directed, presumably used the same actions as they
had always used. The wave of Protestantism
which passed over England, partly as the result of
the Smithfield burnings, had a disastrous effect
on the retention of ceremonial, but it was revived
by Andrewes, Laud, and the Caroline divines,
and never died out. It sprang into fresh life as
one of the fruits of the Oxford Movement.

The whole effect of Catholic worship is cumu-
lative and its appeal largely subconscious. Its
appeal is partly to the historic sense, since its
prayers and ceremonial testify to continuity with a
remote past. It is partly symbolical and is meant
to teach through the eye. It is also aesthetic.
Through it God, who is the God of beauty, as
well as the God of Holiness, appeals to the sense
of beauty in man. A beautiful service with
beautiful music in a beautiful building is a powerful witness to God in men who have eyes with
which to see and ears with which to hear, and
may witness most powerfully to the reality and
mystery of God.

The aesthetic appeal is, therefore, important.
The appeal of architecture, music, and ceremonial

has a legitimate place in our religious economy.
It must, however, be distinguished from the
appeal to emotion, and has no intellectual appeal
at all. Aesthetic feeling is not mere sentiment. The " uplift " given by noble architecture,
splendid music, fine and historic ceremonial, has a
distinct intellectual tinge and is not to be confused
with the sentimental emotionalism aroused by
certain hymns, and tunes, and pictures. Feeling
is not excluded, but it is feeling brought under the
influence of reason. When we condemn things
as " sentimental " or emotional we condemn
them not because they touch the emotions but
because their appeal is *exclusively* emotional, and
reason is banished. So-called sentimental pictures, images, stained-glass windows, hymns and
tunes are condemned because their sole appeal is
to the emotions.

We cannot avoid the appeal to the eye. A
Congregationalist Minister writing on Psychological Considerations of Worship argues that
this appeal is inevitable. " The Word of God,"
he says, "is mediated to us through phenomena—
through presentations to the senses, chiefly the
visual and the auditory." He takes the sacred
monogram in Mansfield College as an illustra-
tion, putting himself in the place of a devout

worshipper, who sees it and says to himself: " 'Son of Man, Son of God, Prince of Peace, Prince of Glory, Shepherd, Brother, Friend, Saviour, Lord, Jesus '—what names, what pictures, surge into the mind, what memories of gracious dealings in the soul." He quotes William Blake who supposes himself to be asked " When the sun rises do you not see a round disk of fire something like a guinea ? " and to reply, " Oh, no ! no ! no ! I see an innumerable company of the heavenly host, crying, ' Holy, holy, holy, is the Lord God Almighty '."

The whole essay is worth attention. Here I need only say that if an ornament, which at best belongs to the region of still life, can so move a devout soul to the apprehension of the divine, how much more the living movement of ordered ceremonial.

Worship, of course, needs words for its expression. Over and above the question whether the words should be intelligible or not, there is a great difference between the Catholic and the Protestant use of them. The Catholic tradition was, and is, to use prayers and service forms of immemorial antiquity. The Protestant tendency was first to discard all the old forms, substituting entirely new devotions, and then to

discard forms altogether and rely on *ex tempore*
prayers and a long sermon which became the
most important part of the service. Bishop
Burnet records that on one occasion in Scotland
the unfortunate Charles II, on a day of devotion,
was required to listen to six sermons, each of them
over an hour long.

The compilers of the Prayer Book, though they
composed new services, and rearranged the old,
drew almost entirely on ancient sources for the
prayers, which Archbishop Cranmer translated
with matchless skill.   There has of late years
been a tendency in non-episcopal circles to use
forms of prayer more freely and in the Church of
England to allow experiments with *ex tempore*
prayers, as witness the Proposed book of 1928,
which allows them at Mattins and Evensong,
" when the service is ended."

Ex tempore prayers, however, have drawbacks.
One chief defect is that, like praying inaudibly,
they make corporate worship more difficult than
it need be.   For the words of a prayer besides
being intelligible should be of such a kind that
the worshipper can make them his own.   The
priest is to some extent a mouthpiece, or spokesman, and should be expressing not merely his
own thoughts and feelings but as far as possible

those of the congregation. The prayers therefore should be in the hands of the congregation
because if the worshipper does not know what is
coming he is in the position of hearing some one
else pray rather than of praying himself. In *ex
tempore* prayer the worshipper too often finds
himself in the position of a listener, rather than an
offerer of prayer, sometimes almost of an in-
voluntary critic.

If he does not know what is coming it is
difficult for him to make the prayer his own. He
is left thinking about some petition when the
offerer of the prayer has gone on to the next
sentence. If he knows the prayer, or has it
before him, he has ample time to enrich it, as it
is offered, with his own intentions, personal
petitions, praise, and thanksgivings. He can—
to use a technical term—mentally farce prayers
out of a book with his own devotions.

This is not to object to the use of *ex tempore*
prayer in public worship altogether. When
people are gathered together for some special
object and have a common need, *ex tempore*
prayer is often the best. Also in mission services
when something very simple is required, unlearned and ignorant folk will often find their
wants expressed by an *ex tempore* prayer, when the

most beautiful prayers out of a book will slide
over their heads without making any impression.
But, for human nature's daily food, for prayers
which have to be heard year in and year out, even
for quite simple folk, it is at least a question
whether the words of a prayer in the Prayer Book,
once they are familiar, will not in the long run be
more satisfactory.

Another thing greatly to be desired in public
prayer is that it should be expressed in words that
make an aesthetic appeal.   It is a great assistance
to the worshipper if the words can appeal by their
beauty to the love of beauty within him.   This is
important.   Among other reasons, because the
words cannot often be changed.   Some tunes
are passable as long as one does not hear them too
often.   Some prayers are first passable, then
tedious, and finally nauseating.   A recent out-
burst on the choice of hymns by an English
Bishop is a case in point.   His lordship moved
beyond endurance by constantly hearing them
has appealed to incumbents to discard for a time
twelve of the most popular hymns in use in
church.   He has heard them so often he cannot bear to hear them again.   But no one,
though he may say them daily, year after year,
ever feels that about the Collects in Morning and

Evening Prayer. Nowhere are to be found prayers more beautifully expressed than in the Book of Common Prayer.

Terseness, lucidity, rhythm, all are there. Good as the Collects are in Latin, Cranmer's English is even better. This is not to say that the Prayer Book services are perfect, or that no revision is needed. But in spite of deficiencies, omissions and dislocations, we have very great reason to be thankful for our Prayer Book, which as a manual of public devotion has no rival in the West.

Looked at in another way the appeal of Catholic worship is indirect, of Protestant direct. Catholic worship relies on a spectacular display, on making use of the historic sense, on music, painting and art, on a sense of mystery in the service itself. All

After writing this, I came across the following passage by Mr. Micklem : *Christian Worship*, p. 194.

" The chief drawback to such extemporary prayer is that it is a very difficult medium for common prayer. If it helps the worshipper to pass beyond the ' phenomenon to God,' it does not make easy his carrying the content of the prayer to God. The mental agility required to grasp the thread of another man's thought as it moves on in a prayer of any continuance, to make it one's own, and to direct it to God is considerable. It is hardly surprising if (as we know from testimony) very many folk have given up the attempt in despair. We have here a main cause of that fatal passivity which is so distressing a characteristic of our congregations to-day. . . . The difficulty of concentrated listening is undeniably very great."

these things find their way subconsciously to the soul. The Protestant appeals directly to the soul; his worship is more consciously rational. What the *Via Media* has done is to retain the essentials of Catholic worship, while by making it audible and intelligible and restoring the sermon, it has given it a better right to be considered a "reasonable service."

4. HOLY ORDERS

The Churches of the *Via Media* have adhered to the historic episcopate, insisting that their ministers should receive authority through the laying on of hands of a duly consecrated bishop; or, to quote the Ordinal of the Church of England:

"No man shall be accounted or taken to be a lawful Bishop, Priest, or Deacon in the Church of England, or suffered to execute any of the said functions, except he be called, tried, examined, and admitted thereunto, according to the Form hereafter following, or hath had formerly Episcopal Consecration or Ordination."

It is to be noticed that the Prayer Book propounds no theory. It gives a practical direction. Now the mediæval theory underlying this insistence on episcopal ordination, was that, as

our Lord commissioned the Apostles, so the
Apostles ordained others—for example Timothy
and Titus—who were to be ordainers in their
turn, so that by a chain of hands, as it were, the
ordained minister reaches back to the Apostles,
and his authority is derived from them. Against
this the followers of Calvin held most strongly
that authority to minister came not from the
laying on of hands but from the choice of the
congregation. John Knox it may be remembered,
though he was already a priest, refused to
minister to the refugees in the Castle of St.
Andrews until given authority by being " *called*."
In the Book of Discipline he did away with the
laying on of hands in ordination, though the
ceremony was restored by Andrew Melville in
1578.[1]

But though the Church of England does not
commit itself to any theory of the Apostolic
Succession, from its careful and deliberate retention of episcopal ordination the mediæval theory
that underlay it seems to be assumed. " It is

[1] " Other ceremony than the public approbation of the people
and the declaration of the chief minister that the person there presented is appointed to serve the church we cannot approve, foralbe it
the apostles used imposition of hands, yet seeing the miracle is ceased
the using the ceremony we judge not necessary." John Knox.
History of the Reformation.

quite true that the Church of England imposes upon the clergy no obligation to hold the dogma that only episcopal ordinations are valid, and only priestly consecrations of the eucharist, and that Bishops are of the *esse* of the Church, but it has acted so far as concerns its corporate action, always in such a way as to satisfy those who hold these doctrines, and to impose a severe restriction on the action which those who do not hold them would naturally wish to take. This, I think, is indisputable. If you hold the Lutheran or the Calvinistic theory of the ministry, you naturally desire to recognize practically the essential indifference of all forms of ministry; but the Church of England by its requirements for ministry most severely restricts such inclination." (C. Gore, *The Basis of Anglican Fellowship*.)

As to whether the traditional theory is borne out by the facts in view of all the evidence that the researches of the last century have brought forth, let me quote Dr. Williams. He writes :[1]

" It will generally be admitted, that the belief in an apostolically descended ministry was universal in the Great Church, at least from the time of St. Augustine onwards. But I venture to think that it is possible without

[1] In *Northern Catholicism*.

unjustifiable dogmatism, to carry back this belief at least a couple of centuries earlier; and in support of this position, I will quote some words from a scholar[1] whose knowledge of primitive Church history was unsurpassed.

"'It does not seem to me open to question even that St. Irenaeus, for instance meant to imply a succession of bishops from the Apostles in such a sense that the bishops inherited not only the Apostles' teaching chair, but also the right to confer the same sacramental gifts as in the first age the Apostles conferred. If the Apostles had (apart from any authority delegated to them from the Church) no such exclusive rights, neither had their successors. But if there were functions which belonged of right to the Apostles, then these functions in so far as they were not peculiar, like the function of bearing witness to the Resurrection, to their own generation, but concerned the permanent spiritual equipment of the Church must have passed on to their successors, unless there was a catastrophic break in the history of Christianity between the apostolic and sub-apostolic periods of which the Church in the second century was wholly unaware.'

"I observe," Dr. Williams goes on to say,

[1] Dr. C. H. Turner.

" that where there is any allusion in the New Testament to the constitution of new Ministers, these are constituted by Apostles or apostolic men. I read of Timothy laying hands upon new presbyters or bishops, and being himself exhorted, to stir up the charisma that was in him by the laying on of St. Paul's hands; and then I turn to the end of the dark period and find much of the system prescribed in the earliest Church orders known to us, and assumed in the earliest writers who make any explicit allusion to the subject. I therefore feel confidence in assuming that the procedure which, as I read the evidence, was in operation at the beginning and end of the ' dark ' period also went on through it—especially as I know no evidence to the contrary. . . .

" If from some vantage point in the open air I notice a train entering a tunnel-mouth on one side of a hill, consisting of seven carriages and if it emerges from the tunnel-mouth on the other side of the hill still consisting of seven carriages, I am entitled to conclude that there was no variation in the number of carriages during the course of its journey through the tunnel."

Cogent as this reasoning may seem to some there are many it will not convince. Two other theories have many champions. One might be described as the delegation theory. Those who hold it argue that the authority of the minister, whether Bishop or Presbyter, if considered as distinct officials, is derived from the congregation, whose delegate in a sense he is. This was the theory of John Knox and is held by the majority of Presbyterians.

We owe the third theory of the ministry to Professor Harnack, who, after the discovery of the *Didache*, maintained the existence of what he called a Charismatic Ministry, on the strength of statements in the *Didache* and two passages in the Epistles of St. Paul. There was, he said, a purely local ministry of presbyter-bishops and deacons, but ranking above them another ministry of prophets, evangelists and teachers, who owed their authority not to any form of ordination but to certain gifts of the Spirit.

Dr. Streeter takes the original ground that all three theories are correct as far as some part of the first century church is concerned. " At the end of the first century A.D.," he writes, " there existed in different provinces of the Roman Empire, different systems of Church Government. Among these, the Episcopalian, the Presbyterian, and the Independent, can each discover the prototype of the system to which he himself adheres. Indeed, if my hypothesis is correct, then in the classical words of Alice in Wonderland, 'Everyone has won, and all shall have prizes'."

Those who hold the transmission theory, therefore, have to face the fact that there are eminent scholars who reject it and that universal agreement is not in sight. It is impossible to produce a *demonstrative* proof in its favour from the New Testament, or the sub-Apostolic Church. Nor is the theory included in any creed, or inculcated in any canon of a General Council. But there is hope that even those who reject the theory underlying episcopacy will accept the practice based on it. The Churches of the Anglican Communion, at least, have never insisted on belief in the theory but only on acceptance of the fact of the historic episcopate as the authorized channel for ordination. But acceptance of the fact is of outstanding importance.

The Archbishop of Canterbury has summed up the position most admirably :

" Various theories," he declared, " have been and are held as to the origins of the episcopacy. But there is no question that by the end of the second century of the Christian era it had secured a place in the life of the Church which even in the midst of the controversies of the fourth and fifth centuries remained unquestioned. Its position historically is analogous to the Canon of Scripture and the Creeds. All alike emerged through a process of gradual growth into a place of accepted authority. Let me quote the words of the Lambeth committee of 1930 : ' If the Episcopate was the result of a like process of adaptation and growth in the organism of the Church, that would be no evidence that it lacked divine authority, but rather that the life of the Spirit within the Church had found it to be the most appropriate organ for the functions which it discharged.' These functions were of great importance to the life and unity of the Church— among them the guardianship of the faith and the Sacraments and the provision of a duly commissioned ministry. Thus—to quote the same report, ' we are persuaded that the historic continuity of the episcopal ministry provides evidence of the divine intention such as to constitute a stewardship which we are bound to discharge '."[1]

5. UNITY

Insistence on episcopal ordination has an added importance because of its bearing on unity. We

[1] Address to Canterbury Diocesan Conference reported in the *Church Times*, July 15, 1934.

I

should all agree that any external symbol of unity is to be valued chiefly on account of the inner spiritual unity which it expresses ; yet some external symbol is necessary and without it spiritual unity is too shadowy and elusive to satisfy the needs of mankind. For the Church has its sphere of operations on earth ; it has to do with men and women who have bodies as well as souls. Its manner of approach is sacramental ; that is, it uses external means to express spiritual realities. It is therefore to be expected that it should express its spiritual unity externally. St. Paul's metaphor of the Body and, indeed, all the words used in the New Testament to describe the Church, such as the Fellowship, the Way, the Ecclesia, point to a unity which could be seen of men, so that it could be said of any one, that he belongs, or does not belong.

When we look for some outward visible sign of unity we have to reckon with the fact that all who are baptized into the one Church are, by that very fact, born into the family. They belong. They may be disinherited, or treat the family as non-existent and cut themselves completely adrift, but they are of it. Nothing can completely sever the link. But baptism by itself is too loose a tie. A certain Shah of

Persia is said to have had over a thousand children. To them the family tie by itself could have meant very little. The baptismal tie, of itself, means in the case of millions even less. It is a foundation stone, which is necessary to the building but of no use if nothing is built on it. We need, in fact, some kind of structural or organic unity if we are to realize our fellowship in Christ, and this Christians are beginning once more to recognize.

The Reformation began a period of disintegration. The Church broke up into several fragments and the fragments became still further subdivided. The twentieth century has witnessed a coming together of broken pieces. The re-union has been chiefly among separated bodies of non-episcopal Protestants, but inter-communion has been established between Anglicans on the one hand and both Old Catholics and the Swedish Church on the other. At least two of the autocephalous churches which compose the Orthodox Church have acknowledged the validity of Anglican Orders, while nearly all are regarding the establishment of inter-communion as a goal which, if still distant, is by no means unattainable. The Conferences, also, between Anglicans and Romans at Malines showed that there exists a

strong desire for reunion among some distinguished members of the Roman Church. The
present generation is at least awake to the sin
and futility of disunion.

What, then, is the common bond or tie which
shall be the outward mark of this organic unity?
Rome insists that it is communion with the
Roman Church—" that by the maintenance of
unity, alike of communion and belief, with the
Roman Pontiff, the Church of Christ may be one
flock under one chief shepherd."

The test is simple, but it is not primitive.
The bond of unity in the Church of the New
Testament was in the Apostles. To be " in the
Apostles teaching and fellowship " was to possess
two of the four distinguishing marks of the infant
Church. It is nowhere suggested that Peter is
the centre of unity. Even when Paul came to
Jerusalem " to make inquiries of Peter " he saw
James as well ; even if we concede for the sake of
argument that Peter was the centre of unity,
there is nothing to show that his functions were to
be transmitted to the Bishop of Rome rather than
held by the whole episcopate. In the New Testament the Apostles form the link which binds
together the scattered parts of the one body.

" The Church "—to quote Canon Lacey—" not

a particular Church, but the Universal Church—is built upon the foundation of the apostolate ; it stands in the Apostles' teaching and fellowship— their travels, their visits, their constant supervision the missions of their delegates, hold the scattered communities together in a social order. And there is more than this. They appoint elders and bishops, officers of familiar style with familiar functions, in the several communities. We naturally infer that only where such officers are appointed will there be a properly constituted Church, representing the whole Church of God. What we read of St. Paul we may surmise of the other Apostles, with whom he freely compares himself, and we can picture a large activity. All depends on the Apostles."[1]

The early Church, indeed, did not need to trouble itself about structural unity. Its dissensions were all on matters of faith. But the Novatianists A.D. 251 and the Donatists sixty years later seceded on questions of discipline. Dr. Williams has pointed out[2] that St. Cyprian was engaged in controversy with the Novatianists and St. Augustine with the Donatists—but that neither invoked fellowship with the Roman

[1] T. A. Lacey, *Unity and Schism*, p. 30.
[2] In *Northern Catholicism*.

Church as the principle of unity. Instead they appealed to numbers. "It is, I venture to think," says Dr. Williams, "an impressive fact that both these champions of the great Church rest the main weight of their case for its claims upon its world-wide diffusion, as contrasted with the local and limited character of the Puritan bodies against which they are arguing." If Rome had been the centre of unity, communion with Rome would have been a simpler and more obvious test to apply. St. Augustine arguing against the Donatists used those words which had such a disastrous effect on Newman when quoted by Wiseman fourteen hundred years later, *securus judicat orbis terrarum*—the whole world judges right.[1] St. Wilfrid used the same argument at the Council of Whitby in 664. "How can you think," he demanded, "that, though your fathers were holy, their small number in a corner of the smallest island is to be preferred before the Church of Christ throughout the world?"

Wilfrid, however, might have been "hoist with his own petard," as the British customs which he opposed, were in part derived from the

[1] Dr. Williams gives the quotation in full. "Securus judicat orbis terrarum quacunque parte terrarum." ep. Parmen. iii. 24. which he translates: "The whole world rightly judges that they are not right who separate themselves everywhere from the whole world."

East and at that date the Orthodox Church of the
East was superior in numbers to the Western
Church, while Newman, when he allowed himself
to be hag-ridden by that fatal sentence, forgot that
whatever force the argument may once have had
was destroyed by the separation of East and West
in 1054 which divided Christendom into two halves.

Two other reasons may be given, which tell
against the papal theory.   One is the existence of
anti-popes.   Between the third century and the
fifteenth there were not less than thirty-six.
The papal theory provides no authority for
adjudicating between the rival claimants.   The
Pope judges all and is judged by none.   When
two men claim to be Pope, who shall judge which
is the rightful Pope?   At the end of the Great
Schism three men each claimed to be Pope.   The
Council of Constance persuaded all three to with-
draw and a fourth was elected.   In any case of a
disputed election it is left to private judgement to
decide which candidate is the lawful Pope.   The
Great Schism lasted thirty-eight years and it was
left to the private judgement of sovereigns to
decide which Pope they would acknowledge.   It
may be said that Providence will prevent such
a state of things, but this is to make unity depend
no longer on the Papacy but on Providence.

The other reason is the failure of the papal theory to prevent schism. Leo XIII declared the papacy to be the indispensable organ of unity; but, if so, it has failed egregiously. Half the Church broke away in 1054. Nearly half the remainder separated at the Reformation. The existence of the Uniate Churches which are the fruit of the Roman theory is a fruitful source of disunion in the Eastern Church. Whatever services the papacy has rendered to the Church, and they are many, the maintenance of Unity can hardly be reckoned one.

To-day, the indispensable condition of reunion is that every minister should be recognized to be such not only by the local Church to which he belongs but by the whole Church. It is not enough for Anglican Orders to be recognized by the Churches of the *Via Media*, they must be recognized universally. The only common ministerial basis there is any hope of establishing is episcopal. I do not judge any other type of ministry. But few will deny that the episcopal was the universal type from about A.D. 170 until the Reformation. Even since the Reformation it has been the type accepted by the great majority of Christendom, by Roman, Anglican, and Orthodox, by Swedish Lutherans and the Old

Catholics. It is difficult to see what other kind is possible as the skeleton, or framework, of a united Church. Bishop Headlam has suggested that the Laying on of Hands with prayer is sufficient for a valid ministry. But this would certainly leave out the Salvation Army and the Friends, while Baptists and Congregationalists would be in a somewhat equivocal position. For though they have retained the Laying on of Hands as a part of Church Order they do not regard it as necessary for the valid celebration of the Sacrament. In principle there seems no real distinction between clerical and lay, except that an ordained minister is recognized as such throughout his denomination.

No other framework of unity than the episcopal seems possible. The inter-communion established between the Church of England and the Old Catholics would have been impossible without this common bond of the Apostolic ministry. The approaches towards union with the great Orthodox Church of the East could not even have begun without it. It is difficult to envisage a reunited Church of the future, with any other than this episcopally transmitted ministry. It is certain that a reunion attempted on any other than an episcopal basis would rend the churches of the Anglican communion from top to bottom, which would be an unfortunate beginning to reunion. Or to quote Bishop Gore once more : " the Anglican Communion would certainly be rent in twain on the day on which any non-episcopally ordained minister was formally allowed within our communion to celebrate the Eucharist."

At the same time we may freely grant that when reunion comes about the Bishop of Rome must be the head of the reunited Church. His primacy would at the least be a primacy of honour. The very size and scale of the re-united Church, makes it difficult to assign any definite function for him to discharge. But as the occupant of the chief see of Christendom, which claims as its founders the two chief apostles, where both were martyred and where their bones still lie ; as the successor of a long line of Popes who during centuries have furnished some of the most distinguished figures in the West, men like Leo the Great, Gregory the Great, Hilde-brand, Innocent III, as the occupant of this see, the Pope has no rival, or competitor, in point of precedence. Though he might lose in *magis-terium* as compared with his present position, in dignity, in influence, in all that constitutes *auctoritas* in its fullest sense he would gain immeasurably.

CHAPTER IV

FREEDOM[1]

" As it is only in a theistic setting that beauty can retain its deepest meaning and love its brightest lustre, so these great truths of aesthetics and ethics are but half truths, isolated and imperfect, unless we add to them a third.   We must hold that reason and the works of reason have their source in God; that from Him they draw their inspiration; and that, if they repudiate their inspiration and origin, by this very act they proclaim their own insufficiency."

LORD BALFOUR, *Gifford Lectures*.

SO much, then, for authority, for that *auctoritas*, or influence, which is rightly brought to bear on the mind and conscience by Scripture and Tradition, interpreting tradition to mean both the past experience and the living judgment of the Church.   But it is necessary to remember that

[1] Perhaps a word of explanation about the sense in which I use the word freedom may be useful.   It is possible of course to include reason and other internal arbiters as co-ordinate *authorities* with Tradition and Scripture, as when one speaks of the " dictates of conscience," or in the same way that St. Paul said, " The love of Christ constraineth me."   But it seems clearer to put all external governance under the heading of authority, and all internal monitions under freedom.

the attitude of the individual towards this influence is not one of blind acquiescence or passive receptivity. He has to test it according to his capacity by the light of reason, conscience, and experience. Side by side with rightful deference to authority there is in the human heart a God-given passion for freedom. It is true that we enter the kingdom of heaven as little children, inquiring eagerly, but accepting on trust knowledge which it is beyond our power to acquire for ourselves. Nevertheless as we grow we develop in varying degrees the desire to test the knowledge which has been given us. This applies to all knowledge. The engineer, the biologist, and the chemist, depend for their advance in knowledge on a kind of interplay between the knowledge that comes to them from others, *given* knowledge that is, and their own individual capacity for comprehending, assimilating, and testing it. In the same way the searcher for truth in religion starts with knowledge which is given him but his progress depends on his power of assimilation, and he should be encouraged to test the knowledge he has received. Here again there is a continual interplay between the knowledge that comes from outside and a man's power of assimilating and testing it.

It is perfectly true that a large number, probably a considerable majority of sincerely religious people, to whatever denomination they belong, never subject their religion to any test. They have taken it from their parents or their teachers, on trust; it has met their needs as they grew up. They believe it helps them; they are not aware of any intellectual chink in its armour; its worship appeals to them. Much the same might be said of many who stumble, as it were by chance, on a church which they eventually join. But they might claim that they have subjected their religion to the most searching test of all, the test of experience.

But there are others who require something more. They may have inquiring intellects; or the religion in which they were brought up may have failed them in their hour of need; or they may be repelled by its worship. Whatever the cause they become seekers.

What then are these inner authorities, the constituent parts of this jury empanelled in a man's own soul, which must wittingly, or unwittingly, test the monitions that come from a source outside himself? They are first the reflective reason, and secondly, intuition or inspiration, whatever its source, and thirdly, experience.

But though it is convenient to consider these three inner authorities one by one, it must be remembered that in actual practice they are almost inseparably bound up together.

I. THE REFLECTIVE REASON

First let us take the reasoning powers of man, by which he compares one theory with another, draws inferences, and arrives at reasoned conclusions, putting, as we say, two and two together. The conclusions may be right or wrong but they are rational, not instinctive. The Catholic doctrine of the Trinity has been hammered out by reason—whether inspired or not by the Holy Spirit is not at the moment in debate. It was never revealed as a complete formula ; nor was it, as far as we know, the result of a sudden inspiration.

It is a mark of the *Via Media* that those who belong to it are welcome to test their religion by their reason and they are not asked to accept anything on authority which seems to them unreasonable. Professor Taylor tells the story of a Roman Catholic who was told of a certain Anglo-Catholic : " He believes everything that you believe." " Yes," was the reply, " but he believes for the wrong reason. He holds the Catholic faith because he believes it to be true, whereas he should be holding it because it is taught by infallible authority." True or not, the story not unfairly illustrates the standpoint of the infallible Church. If it is right to take your religion on trust and because some authority outside yourself tells you it is true it is wrong to question its truth, once you have accepted it. Its votaries may investigate it and discover reasons and arguments in its favour but always on the assumption that they do not permit ourselves to doubt its truth.

I contend on the contrary that it is contrary to the spirit of truth to fetter the inquiring mind. It must be free to come to whatever conclusion seems to it to be true. It is the glory of *Via Media* that in spite of its leaning on authority it allows scope and freedom to the inquirer. The mental attitude of the whole-hearted authoritarian is illustrated by a question is a well-known devotional manual. " Have I," the priest is told to ask himself. " Have I through faith made a sacrifice of my reason to God, by believing whatever has been held in the Catholic Church, *semper, ubique et ab omnibus* ? "

This attitude is contrary to the genius of the *Via Media*. The doubting Thomas has a moral right to face his doubts and follow his argument wherever it may lead him ; even if it leads him away from the faith of the Church we do not condemn, but believe that if he is honest and sincere and looks far enough he will in due time regain the truth. Man in the last resort has to decide as best he can in religion as in worldly affairs mainly by the light of his reason. " I could never endure," wrote Charles Gore, in his last great book, " to be otherwise than a free-thinker. I mean by that that whatever obligation I may have inherited, or contracted, to any traditional system of belief or thought, I could never allow it to blind me to anything which might seem to be truth, whatever its origin or to shackle me so that I could not follow the light of reason whithersoever it lead."

It has been objected that the English Churchman is compelled to reason in fetters, because he is bound by the creeds and the Bible. This is, of course, so far true inasmuch as if he rejects the creeds he can hardly in honesty retain office in the Church. But could a Presbyterian minister, who believed in the necessity of Episcopacy, or a Wesleyan who rejected the doctrine of the Atonement, or a Baptist who insisted on infant Baptism, or a Unitarian who believed in the divinity of Christ, retain office in their respective denominations ?

There is, indeed, a tendency in some quarters at the present day to disparage the reason as a means of arriving at truth in religion. " Critics of the twentieth century," wrote a reviewer[1] in 1924, " had grown out of the rationalistic age in which Dr. Gore still dwelt ; they had learned that religion neither could, nor need, have any rational justification, but had its own canons and its own justification." The reviewer seems to be writing under the influence of Otto and Barth, who have headed a reaction in Germany against the over-rationalization of religion, making it depend too exclusively on the reflective reason.

There is, of course, an inspirational element in religion, as we shall see later, which we accept without being able to give a reason for the decisions it leads us to make. We also have to remember that when the reason has done its best and summed up all the arguments for and against, there still remains something wanting. There is, in fact, a gap between argument and decision which has to be crossed by faith. Faith is the element in

[1] Quoted by Canon Hodgson, *The Place of Reason in Christian Apologetics*, from the *Church Times*.

K

man which makes him accept some tenet as sufficiently established for him to act upon, before he
has rational proof of it. Nevertheless it is
suicidal to disparage the work of the reflective
reason in religion. The decay of worship since
the war is largely due to the fact that belief in
Christianity is considered by a very large number,
probably a majority, of educated people to be
irrational. Young people to-day are not content
to be told that morals and religious truths are
taught by the Church or found in the Bible. They
will not accept them unless they commend
themselves to the reason and the moral sense.
" The younger generation," said a speaker at a
Youth Conference the other day, " no longer says,
' Does the Church or the Bible teach it ? ' but ' Is
it true ? ' " Indeed most educated people feel
that in the last resort no religion can command
their whole-hearted allegiance unless it appeals
to their heads as well as their hearts, to their
reason as well as their feelings.

The Witness of History.

The History of the Church affords abundant
evidence that the reflective reason has its rights.
Our Lord did as we have seen appeal to authority,
but He clearly sought to convince the intellect

as well as to elicit faith. He bade his followers
count the cost of discipleship, and He adopted
the parabolic method of teaching in order to make
them think. His rebuke to the two disciples on
the way to Emmaus after the Resurrection was a
rebuke for slowness of perception, as well as
want of faith. They were " fools " as well as
" slow of heart to believe." After expounding
the scriptures He said " ought not Christ to
have suffered ? " In other words He appealed to
their reason. In other Resurrection appearances
He appealed to them to reason on the evidence of
their senses. He sought to convince the disciples
of the reality of His risen body by bidding them
handle His body and invited Thomas to feel His
hands and the hole in His side. By so doing He
invited them to make rational inferences. When
the beloved disciple entered the tomb and behold-
ing the grave-clothes " saw and believed," he also
made a rational inference from the appearance of
the clothes and the position of the napkin. However much St. Paul claims to lay aside the use of
the enticing words of man's wisdom, he certainly
appeals to men's reason, as well as to their faith.
A modern novelist writing from a detached point
of view has described St. Paul as " an argumentative zealot." He may, or may not, have been a

zealot. He was certainly argumentative, and arguments are addressed to the reason.

Justin Martyr claimed philosophy as an aid to Christianity and philosophy implies reasoning. Tertullian it is true repudiated reason, declaring that Greek science was the invention of devils, but Tertullian was a hot-headed zealot, who went over to Montanism. His opinions, nevertheless, found sympathizers at Alexandria. There they were called Orthodoxasts and their watchword was "Only believe." But Clement who became Head of the Catechetical School at Alexandria and his disciples, while professing entire loyalty to the Christian faith, eagerly enlisted in its support all human philosophy and learning. They argued that philosophy was the handmaid of religion. They agreed with the Orthodoxasts that Scripture was inspired but their great Platonic maxim, that nothing was to be believed which was unworthy of God, makes reason the judge of Revelation. Origen, indeed, Clement's great disciple, met the charge of despising wisdom, which was brought against Christians, with a passionate denial, and vindicated St. Paul from the charge of depreciating it.

From about A.D. 500–1100 Western Europe

was plunged into the darkness of barbarism and reason was under a cloud. Nevertheless, it was not left without its champions. John Scotus Erigena, the witty Irishman, who was murdered by his pupils at Malmesbury in the reign of King Alfred, argued that " all authority which is not approved by true reason seems weak " and was censured by Florus, a contemporary, for presumption as " daring to define with his own reason what should be held and followed." St. Bernard and Abelard afforded a classic instance of the conflict between the champions of authority and reason. Peter Abelard declared that " a doctrine is not to be believed because God has said it but because we are convinced by reason that it is so."

The great age of the Schoolmen was an heroic attempt on the part of theologians, like St. Thomas Aquinas (1225–1274) to vindicate the rights of reason in religion, though it must be admitted that, at least by his day, the stake was the appointed end of those whose reason brought them to any but an orthodox conclusion.

The Reformation was in one sense an appeal to reason. For it was an appeal against usurped and unjust authority, which implies the power of judging and discriminating, and therefore of

exercising reason, but by its authors it was
considered to be not so much an appeal from
authority to reason, as an appeal from one
authority to another, from the authority of the
Church to the authority of the Scripture.

Luther, in fact, distrusted reason in religion as
much as any papist. He called it " the devil's
harlot." " To Luther the sacrifice (of reason)
was the condition of feeling the normal power of
God while to Erasmus its complete blending
with the soul was the way to Catholic truth. We
must distinguish, according to Luther, between
our relations with God and our relations with the
world. In the first capacity the Holy Spirit
reigns, and Reason is only a courtezan " (Frau
Hulda). " Luther," comments R. H. Murray,[1]
" is anxious to offer up to God will, intellect,
and activity, as a reasonable sacrifice. We must
destroy our reason in order to be born of the
Spirit."

When Protestants who had rejected the oracular authority of the Pope were busy trying to set
up the oracular authority of the Bible, and
substituting Geneva for Rome, Richard Hooker
in his *Ecclesiastical Polity* sought to establish
Anglicanism on a surer basis. While maintaining

[1] *Erasmus and Luther.*

the authority of Scripture and of Tradition he
insisted that a third factor must be taken into
account, the human reason.   A large part of the
Ecclesiastical Polity is devoted to the vindication
of the use of reason in theology as against the
Puritan theory of the sufficiency of the inspired
word of Scripture.   It is to be noticed that in
defending the use of reason he is arguing against
Geneva, not Rome.   His "whole theory,"
says Dean Church, " rests on the principle that
the paramount and supreme guide both of
the world and of human action is *reason*."

Hooker insists[1] that however *faith* comes
to man, whether by revelation, or instruction, or
the secret inspiration of the Holy Ghost, the
knowledge is impossible " without discourse
of natural reason." Without reason we could
not reap the benefit of Scripture.   " The word of
God is a two-edged sword but (only) in the hands
of reasonable men."   He complains[2] that " the
star of reason and learning was beginning
to be thought of as it were as an unlucky comet,
and esteemed like the star in the book (of
Revelation) called Wormwood."   "A number
there are," he asserts, " who think they cannot
admire as they ought the power and authority of

[1] *Ecclesiastical Polity*, III, 8.   [2] *Ibid.*

the Word of God, if in things divine they should attribute any force to man's Reason. For which cause they never use reason so willingly as to disgrace reason." "An opinion hath spread itself very far in the world," he complained, "as if the way to be ripe in faith were to be raw in wit and judgment; as if Reason were an enemy unto religion, childish simplicity the mother of ghostly and divine wisdom."

In thus exalting reason Hooker was in advance of his time. The High Churchmen of the school of Andrewes and Laud, who built up the Anglican tradition on Hooker's foundation during the next fifty years, were chiefly concerned to establish the claims of Church authority against those who denied it, and were champions of tradition, not reason. But the High Churchmen although temporarily eclipsed by the Civil War and the martyrdoms of William Laud and Charles I, received their real check from the Latitudinarians, who headed a reaction in favour of reason against the authority alike of Church and Scripture. William Chillingworth inaugurated this new era, in which the Cambridge Platonists were the brightest stars. Its later adherents, however, tended to depend too exclusively on the ratiocinative reason, and to belittle faith and inspiration. They appealed too much to the head and too little to the heart. In consequence their coldness and dryness led to the Evangelical Movement which exalted feeling at the expense of reason.

Partly in protest against the Evangelicals, but principally as an aftermath of the French *Age of Reason* there was a powerful, if not very numerous party in England in the early part of the nineteenth century, which was inclined to reject every authority in religion except that of reason. Jeremy Bentham and the Utilitarians with their slogan, as some people would call it now, of the greatest happiness of the greatest number, were of this way of thinking. Newman called them Liberals, and said that the essence of liberalism consisted in " the anti-dogmatic principle." The Tractarians, indeed, came into the field to fight Liberalism. Their controversy with Evangelicals was later. All the first leaders, Keble, Newman himself, Froude and Pusey, were sworn foes of Liberalism and distrusted the use of reason in religion.

Liddon was in the same tradition as the pioneers of the movement, but there had already appeared signs of revolt, notably in the cases of J. B.

Mozley and Richard Church. It was for this reason that Church was out of sympathy with Pusey even before he became Dean of St. Paul's, and not long after he left Oxford definitely refused to be reckoned as one of Pusey's party. One great service that Charles Gore rendered to the Church was to vindicate the rights of reason in religion, as he did all his life, but notably in *Lux Mundi* a collection of Essays of which he was Editor and principal contributor. It was published in 1889 and announced to the world that the Tractarian lamb was prepared to lie down with the Liberal lion and that at least a *modus vivendi* between reason and authority had been found. For in it the Editor, Charles Gore, let it be understood that its contributors were prepared to accept the results of modern criticism and to reconcile revelation with the evolutionary theories of Charles Darwin. Verbal inspiration went by the board. Newman had in 1837 condemned " the exercise of thought upon matters in which from the constitution of the human mind, thought cannot be brought to any successful issue and is therefore out of place," but few Anglo-Catholics would accept his position to-day.

Reason has its rights in religion as in science, though religion has to reckon with factors that science can ignore.   If we believe in the Christian religion at all we must believe there are things in it we could not find out for ourselves by the power of our unaided reason ; nevertheless we are not required to sacrifice our reason in the sense of believing that which we think unreasonable, or to refuse to exercise it on religious matters for fear it should make us doubt.

2. INSPIRATION OR INTUITION

The second internal authority we may call loosely inspiration or intuition.   A thought comes unbidden into the mind without any exercise of our reasoning powers of which we are aware.   It may be the result of some sub-conscious process of the mind ; it may be the direct inspiration of the Holy Ghost.   "He that believeth in the Son hath the witness in himself." Yet God is a God who hideth Himself, and it is often difficult to distinguish between intuition, or the result of the undirected working of our own brain, and inspiration proper, by which we mean a direct suggestion from outside.

When overawed by some magnificence in nature, or the beauty of a building, or a service, the thought " Surely God is in this place," may come unbidden, without any process of reasoning.

" Just when we are most sure, there's a sunset touch,
    A fancy from a flower-bell, someone's death
A chorus—ending from Euripides,
    And that's enough for fifty hopes and fears
As old and new at once as nature's self,
    To rap and knock and enter into our soul."

Our aesthetic judgements are largely intuitional. There is, of course, a scientific and intellectual side to aesthetics, but for most people the appeal is primarily intuitive. They are drawn to a particular form of worship because it appeals to their sense of beauty, but they could not explain why it appeals to them. Englishmen are disinclined to admit this motive but it exists. A man goes to a particular service because, as he says, he feels he gets more good there. He sometimes means that it appeals to his sense of beauty. The growth in ceremonial, in music, and in church decoration during the last hundred years has not been entirely the outcome of deference to tradition, and still less as the result of hard reasoning. These may be subsidiary causes but the *causa causans*, the *fons et origo*, is the love of beauty for its own sake. The vast improvement that has occurred in these respects in the last few years is due to the frank recognition of the claims of

beauty as having a rightful place in our religious
life, and, as a corollary, that religion has a right
to the best that art can give.

Otto and Barth have done a great service in
laying stress on the importance of inspiration.
For Otto's teaching on the apprehension of the
Numinous, and Barth's on the acceptance of the
Word of God, imply inspiration, since the thought
comes into the mind apparently unbidden and
from outside.   Whether we attribute such
intuitions or experiences to the direct inspiration
of the Holy Ghost, or to the Holy Ghost acting
on the subconscious reason, is unimportant.   It
is enough for us to believe that there are intuitions
which come from God and not as the result of
conscious ratiocination.   They seem to come of
themselves : we do not think them out as far as
we know. To deny that there are such inspirations is to deny the history of our religion.
When St. Paul " essayed to go into Bithynia "
" the spirit suffered him not." The decisive
moment in the long history of St. Augustine's
conversion was the voice he heard when lying
under the tree, saying, " *tolle lege*."

Our moral judgements are often intuitive.
When we say our conscience tells us we ought to
do, or refrain from doing something our decision

may be the result of intuition, or of a process of reasoning.

The point arises as to what control, if any, can be exercised by the recipient of these inspirations. How can he check them so as to know if they are from God or are merely the results of the working of the undirected mind ? Can the individual who believes he is inspired claim for himself that his inspiration overrides all authority and is subject to no control ? The Montanist prophets in the third century of our era made such a claim. The Anabaptists split from Lutherans and Calvinists alike on this point, by insisting on the plenary authority of their own inspirations. They loved to contrast what they called the dead letter of scripture with the living voice of the Spirit, very much to the disadvantage of Scripture. Calvin called them " this vermin " in consequence The early Quakers at home and in New England did many extravagant things, pleading a similar authority. So did Joan of Arc who insisted that she must obey the " voices " she heard, and was burnt for claiming that they came from God. Richard Baxter, the Puritan, says that many of the Quakers, his contemporaries, wandered about naked, and drowned themselves out of melancholy, alleging the voice of the Spirit as their authority for such eccentric behaviour. "They" (the Quakers) said Baxter, "make the light that every-man hath within him a sufficient rule." In the same way "the Ranters," he says, "made it their business to set up the Light of Nature under the name of Christ in man and to dishonour and cry down the Church, Scriptures, ministry, worship and ordinances." The Behemists likewise were "for the sufficiency of the Light of Nature."

Experience, however, has taught the most enthusiastic sects that their votaries unless subject to some control cannot be restrained from absurdities. To-day no important body allows oracular authority to the individual inspiration of the Holy Spirit. All agree that some kind of check is necessary. "The Friends lay much emphasis on the importance of testing one's insight by convincing the spiritual group of fellow-members of its truth and quality, but they put much more importance on the test of life. Is the conviction, the insight, the urge, one that fits in well with the tested laws and principles of life and character?"[1] What is this but to test inspiration by the reason?

Members of the Group Movement attach the greatest importance to the direct guidance of the

---

[1] *The Faith and Practice of the Quakers*, Rufus Jones, p. 53.

Holy Spirit, but they recommend that individual guidance should be checked in doubtful cases by the guidance given to other members of the Group. When we compare results and balance one with the other we make reason the judge, whether with the Groups and the Pietists generally we make inspiration our chief guiding star, or whether we agree with Richard Hooker that "we are on a plainer ground when we gather by reason from the quality of things believed or done, that the Spirit of God hath directed us in both, than if we settle ourselves to believe or do any particular thing, as being moved thereto by the Spirit." But in either case we admit the claims of reason. However ready therefore we are to acknowledge the divine origin of intuition we do not exclude the operation of reason. Because it is our reason, as must be the case with rational beings, which has the last word.

We must, however, claim insistently the guidance of the Spirit in the work of the reason. As Christians we maintain that the Holy Spirit helps us in those decisions to which we come after praying for God's blessing and in submission to His will. When St. James at the Council of Jerusalem said—"It seemed good to the Holy Ghost and to us," he spoke of a reasoned conclusion arrived at after discussion. Hooker insists on this inspiration of the reason. "There are but two ways," he wrote, "whereby the Spirit leadeth man into all truth; the one extraordinary, the other common; the one belonging but unto some few, the other extending itself unto all that are of God; which we call by a special divine excellency Revelation, the other reason."

The Church has, indeed, always sought heavenly guidance in its formal conciliar and reasoned decisions. The Orthodox Church pays less heed to the decisions than to their subsequent reception. Here the Easterns seem to be on a truer line of development in preferring to find the working of the Spirit in a general movement of the whole body rather than in clear-cut decisions. This is certainly the method of Anglicanism. We believe that in the labour of the scholar, the judgements of a Council, the new light shed on God's dealings with us by the growth of the spirit of humanity which has made us revise our ideas of God, in all these the Holy Spirit has been inspiring and guiding. To take only one point. In the year 1859 the devout were horrified because in Essays and Reviews the eternity of hell-fire seemed to be called in question, and by hell most people meant a place of physical

L

torment.   Most devout people would to-day be equally horrified if told that such a hideous doctrine was part of the Christian faith.   Yet there has been no voice of authority from the Church, or any large part of it, repudiating such a belief, nor has anyone direct divine inspiration for denying it.   It seems to me a clear instance of the guiding and inspiring work of the Spirit of God acting not on one individual or one Council but touching the hearts of multitudes of believers and bringing them to their right mind.   Therein seems to lie the hope of the future.

3. EXPERIENCE

When Philip said to Nathanael, in reply to his question, " Can any good thing come out of Nazareth ? " " Come and see," he was inviting him to apply the test of experience.   When the men of Sychar who said to the woman who talked to Jesus at the well, " Now we believe not because of thy word but because we have seen Him and know for ourselves that this is the Christ, the Son of God," they were appealing to the same test.   All religious people are experimenters.   Prayer is a real part of our lives and, however different from the answers we hoped or expected, if we do not get any answers that are recognizably answers, our religion is undermined. If we never pray in the sense of really expecting an answer we can hardly be said to have lived as Christians at all.

This appeal to religious experience involves both reason and inspiration. By religious experience we usually mean the knowledge we have of the power of God, as shown in answers to prayer and in other ways, our experience of religion as satisfying a want, in bringing pardon, peace, and joy into life. For instance, I may say "I have found by experience that prayer is answered. Therefore I believe in Prayer." "I attend High Mass, or I make my communion weekly, and I find it helps me, therefore although I cannot answer your objections I shall continue to go." Such drawing upon experience implies the use of both reason and intuition in varying degrees.

Over and above what we may call the humdrum experience of the ordinary Christian the great mystics have in every age believed that there are moments in which the soul has immediate apprehension of God. In such moments, of course, reason is quiescent, yet if any practical action is taken as a result reason is called in. I can illustrate this by an incident which a friend of mine now gone to his rest,[1] once related to me, though he would be horrified by finding himself associated by implication with the great mystics. At one time, when he was an undergraduate of Trinity College, Cambridge, his mind was torn with doubts about the truth of the Christian religion. One day when out for a solitary walk he had a vision of our Lord walking by his side. He always believed that the vision was a reality sent to assure him, and said that from that hour he had no more doubts. Now my friend's interests outside theology were in natural science. He had gone up to Cambridge to study for the medical profession. He always retained his scientific interests. It is absurd to think that he did not apply his reason to the consideration of the vision. Indeed he could not have acted on it without using his reason, as no word was spoken. He was left to make inferences, which were of course rational.

There is also and this is most important, the experience of Christian conduct in daily life : for most of us there are not many occasions when we can say, " Here God has given a definite answer to my prayer." The mystic sense of communion comes to few even once in a lifetime. But if we

[1] Thomas Claude Robson, late Dean of Kimberley.

give ourselves whole-heartedly to do God's will, and find that peace and joy follow, and that the more whole-heartedly we do it the more abundant the peace and joy, experience shows that the Christian life is the right life.

Private Judgement.

But if we are going to leave the final decision to this interior jury, whether reason, intuition, and experience has the predominating voice, we bring in the principle of private judgment, and private judgment is anathema to all Roman and to a great many English Catholics. The Tractarians when the Movement began were so impressed by the conflicting opinions and contradictory interpretations of Scripture among Protestants, that they hoped to oppose individual and eccentric opinions with the judgement of the Church to which individuals must defer.

Newman, who was always seeking certainty in religion, thought, as we have seen, that with regard to Scripture, the Church like another Daniel must provide both the correct text and its interpretation. Dr. Pusey and the other Tractarian leaders were more cautious. They were agreed in thinking that where there was a consensus of opinion among the fathers on any disputed point they were bound by that opinion. But this appeal to learning necessarily allows room for a good deal of private judgment. For, as Abelard showed long ago, there is considerable diversity of opinion among the Fathers even on important points. When the doctors differ it must be left to private judgement to decide between them.

It seems doubtful if this renunciation of private judgement even among Roman Catholics, is as complete as they believe it to be, and whether it is any more possible to renounce entirely private judgement in religion than in secular affairs. We may normally defer to the judgement of the Church as expressed by its officers as we may defer to our banker or stockbroker in finance, or to our doctor on a point of medicine, or to an eminent biologist on some question of heredity. The difficulty is that experts often differ. We are dissatisfied and take another opinion, and when this differs from the first we may procure a third which need not agree with either of the other two. Finally we have to act as a jury and after hearing the reasons decide for ourselves. There is no way out.

So in religion. It is true that many, probably a majority, are quite willing to accept what their teachers tell them to believe. They are like the

lady who is content to let her solicitor see to her
investments and trusts him implicitly, not invari-
ably with the happiest results. But if the
teachers differ they must decide for themselves.
In any case every convert must choose his
teacher by an act of private judgement, and even
when he has submitted, if ever doubts rise in
his mind he has to judge for himself whether he
can still abide by the judgement of the Church.
Keble thought that Manning and his friends
deceived themselves in thinking that they escaped
the exercise of private judgement by joining the
Roman Church. "How then," he wrote to Dr.
Pusey in 1850, "is the individual not the judge
of the church both present and past if he deter-
mines on his private judgement that such and such
are the marks of the church and that such and such
a body has them. It may be right or wrong but
surely it is private judgement."

Even those who are in the Roman obedience
must if faced by a difficult question, whether
aware of it or not, exercise private judgement.
If a Roman Catholic is asked, for instance, if it
is ever right to burn heretics alive, and inwardly
revolted by the thought of such cruelty, feels
bound to answer—"no." He has exercised his
judgement in preferring his own humanity to the

opinion of the Church. Again, what test is there in the last resort of the infallibility of a papal decision, except private judgement, a sufficiently weighty matter one would think to have to decide.

The fact is we cannot do away with private judgement. The most loyal and submissive Anglican may find that, though on most important points the judgement of the Church is clear, yet on many points there is no universal agreement, such as on the marriage question, while on others, such as the text and the interpretation of Scripture, new knowledge is continually being added to our stores.

Judging by the letters that have appeared in the *Church Times* for some months, a large number of Anglo-Catholics hold that participation in any war is forbidden to a Christian. Others as stoutly defend participation in certain kinds of war. Both sides quote early Christian writers and Canons but draw diametrically opposite conclusions. The humble layman who reads these effusions can only decide by an exercise of private judgement. It is a question of degree. The non-Catholic Protestant tends to glory in not deferring to Church tradition or authority; he is suspicious of any opinion which he thinks is not founded on private judgement. The Roman Catholic on the other hand regards private judgement as anathema, repudiates it in theory, and only resorts to it in practice under necessity, and, as it were, by stealth. The middle way is better. To regard with respect the judgement of the Church, its worship, its creed and its tradition, and to defer to them, but not in so slavish a manner that the inquirer does not feel free to look these gift horses in the mouth and test them by the light of his own reason, his moral sense and his experience. It is our glory, not our shame.

CHAPTER V

GOVERNMENT

BESIDES the authority (*auctoritas*) we have been considering, as one of the principal foundations of belief, there is another kind of authority, that of government, or discipline, with which no corporate body can dispense. The ancient Romans called it *imperium*; modern Rome calls it *magisterium*. Authority in the sense of *auctoritas* tells us what to believe; authority in the sense of *magisterium* tells us how to act; one is mainly concerned with theory, the other with practice, though it is necessary to remember that in the end practice is based on belief. When we consider authority as *magisterium* we see that it is exercised in three ways: it is legislative, exercising authority to make laws; it is judicial, exercising authority to interpret them, or it is executive, exercising authority to carry them out.

Here, again, we are confronted with the gigantic claims of Rome. If these claims can be made good then *cadit quaestio*. For Rome claims to be not only the mother but also the mistress of all Churches, and that the Pope derives his magisterial authority, as much as his authority to define doctrine from Christ through Peter. He is the ultimate repository of all magisterial authority. " He judges all ; he is judged of none." Even the powers which Bishops receive at their consecration can only be exercised when the Pope confers on them *jurisdiction*, which can be recalled at his will, and which needs to be renewed at regular intervals. Recently the Pope sent to the Archbishop of Rheims to demand his resignation. After being duly consecrated and admitted to his office, he was required to vacate it without a trial before any legal tribunal on receipt of a message from the Pope. Could autocracy go further ?

In face of the tremendous claims made by Rome for its pontiff we have to ask—" By what authority doest thou these things and who gave thee this authority ? " Is the power of God or of man ? The question is of course closely linked with the claim to speak with infallible, or at least oracular, authority. The power whose opinions may not be discussed is likely to issue autocratic commands. If it is immoral to question the Pope's opinion it is equally immoral to disobey his command. Infallibility and autocracy walk hand in hand. Neither in Russia, Italy, nor Germany, where autocracy prevails, is any free expression of opinion allowed. That is not surprising, but it is a shock to find that Mr. H. G. Wells in *The Shape of Things to Come*, where he outlines the lineaments of the future world state, will tolerate no free expression of opinion. He explains that the new world government will not brook the competition of rival religious systems. It will have no place for Christianity. There must henceforth be one faith only in the world, "the moral expression of the one world community."

The question is whether this papal autocracy is ordained by God, or whether it has developed like any other form of government as the result of the play of natural forces, so that it may be judged on its merits and not be taken as something sacrosanct and above criticism. Except for one text already considered it is difficult to find even the germ of the papal autocracy in the New Testament. There is nothing else in the gospels that even suggests it. "As my father hath sent me, even so send I *you* (plural)," was our Lord's commission, not to St. Peter, but to the Apostles. It is the Apostles who are to sit on twelve thrones judging the twelve tribes of Israel. No one of them is to be called Lord or Master. Our Lord, indeed, seems to go out of

His way to show that the supreme *magisterium* after His own departure was to rest with the apostolate as a whole.

It is the same after the Ascension. It is true that St. Peter takes the lead in the choice of a successor to Judas, in preaching to the crowd on the day of Pentecost, in addressing the Sanhedrin, and on other occasions. St. Peter plainly was the leader of the apostolic band. His actions are those of one who possesses initiative. He proposes; he suggests; he takes the lead. Nevertheless acts expressing the deliberate will of the whole Church and belonging to the province of a sovereign authority issue from the whole body of Apostles. If Peter urges the Church to appoint a successor to Judas "they" appointed the two, who were to be drawn by lot. In the ordination of the seven, "the twelve" called the disciples together, and bade them look out seven men of good report—" whom *they* set before the Apostles, and when *they* had prayed *they* laid their hands on them." At the first Council, James was the President—not Peter. When the Apostles at Jerusalem heard of the baptisms in Samaria " *they* sent unto them Peter and John," which is hardly the way one would describe a visitation by a sovereign pontiff.

When St. Paul paid his first visit to Jerusalem after his conversion he tells us that his object was " to see Peter," using a word for " to see," which means properly, as Dr. C. H. Turner has pointed out, to " make inquiries of." Surely a very natural proceeding. A new convert, who had been converted in such an extraordinary way, would naturally make some inquiries, if only about our Lord's life in the flesh, and the chief Apostle was the person to whom he would naturally go. It is noteworthy that he mentions that he also saw James. When fourteen years later St. Paul paid his second visit to Jerusalem, the Jewish question was getting decidedly difficult. This visit was more formal and official, and he took with him Barnabas and Titus. It was also important, for he says he went up by revelation. What did he do ? " I laid before *them* the gospel which I preach among the Gentiles, but privately before *them* who were of repute, lest by any means I should be running, or had run in vain." Here there is no mention of Peter, or any single Apostle, but those " who were of repute." He continues : " they I say who were of repute imparted nothing to me : but contrariwise when they saw that the gospel of the uncircumcision was committed unto me as the gospel

of the circumcision was to Peter ... and when they
saw the grace that was given unto me, James and
Cephas and John, they who were reputed to be
pillars, gave to me and Barnabas the right hands
of fellowship ; that we should go to the heathen
and they unto the circumcision." Here the
three are linked together and James (the Lord's
brother) is first as he was at the Council at Jerusalem.   Later on, when Peter came to Antioch
" I withstood him," says St. Paul, " to the face
because he was to be blamed."

Taking the whole passage it is plain that each of
the three was a leader, but no one of them was a
sovereign pontiff.   There is no hint of autocracy
in I Peter : which is the least authoritative
epistle in the New Testament.   In the Apocalypse the names of the twelve Apostles are
written in apparent equality on the twelve
foundation stones of the new Jerusalem.

The origin of the papal autocracy is to be found
not in the New Testament, but in the secular
Roman Empire.   Autocracy was taken for
granted in the State, and it seemed equally right
and proper in the Church.   " If a man consider
the original of this great ecclesiastical dominion
he will easily perceive that the papacy is no other
than the ghost of the deceased Roman Empire,

sitting crowned upon the grave thereof." When
Constantine removed the seat of Empire to
Constantinople even the western Emperors ceased
to reside in Rome, before long becoming merely
puppet Emperors, and in 476 ceasing altogether.
The Bishop of Rome was not overshadowed by
the Emperor as was the Patriarch of Constantinople in that city, and automatically became the
chief personage in Rome.

From about A.D. 400 for some two hundred
years the Roman Empire in the West was in a
state of dissolution. Successive waves of barbarians broke on its frontiers, overflowed its
boundaries, and submerged its civilization. The
European nations, as we know them to-day,
were eventually to emerge out of the welter,
but the process of development was slow and
was preceded by a period of disintegration,
upheaval, and anarchy, which lasted for many
centuries. During all this time the great
majority of men and women urgently felt the
need of a centre of political, moral and social
authority, such as secular Rome had once been
and was no longer ; the only hope or prospect of
any such centre seemed to be in the Pope. Sick
of anarchy, people looked back to the autocracy
of the Roman Emperors as to a golden age, and

in the autocracy of the Pope saw some hope of a revival of order.

I do not think that we can consider the papal autocracy to have been established before the days of the great Hildebrand, who became Pope in 1073, after being the power behind the throne from at least 1059. But for the weakness and crimes of so many of the individuals who occupied the papal throne, the autocracy might have been established much earlier.

The first attempt to claim a world-wide authority was made A.D. 190 by Victor when he excommunicated the Eastern Churches for keeping Easter on the day of the Jewish Passover. This act brought upon him the rebukes of many Bishops, including Irenaeus, who, according to Eusebius, the fourth-century historian, " Censured Victor with unusual severity," Eusebius himself being plainly unaware that they were censuring a sovereign pontiff.

Canon XXVIII of the Oecumenical Council of Chalcedon A.D. 451 stated : " The fathers gave properly privileges to the throne of old Rome, because it was the imperial city : the 150 Bishops moved with the same intention, gave equal privileges to the most holy throne of new Rome (i.e., Constantinople), judging with reason that the

M

city which was honoured with the sovereignty,
and senate, and enjoyed equal privileges with the
elder imperial Rome should also be magnified
like her in ecclesiastical matters being the second
after her." Nothing can be plainer than that the
fathers of Chalcedon who enacted this canon in
the teeth of the protests of the Roman legates
did not regard the privileges of Rome as part of
the divine and essential constitution of the
Church. We know also that the acceptance of
Roman authority was greatly helped by forgeries.
" We may not be able," wrote Bishop Gore, " to
fix on any individuals the responsibility for such
forgeries as the Donation of Constantine and the
Isidorian Decretals but it goes against our
surest instincts to believe that a system, which was
corresponding in its actual method of working to
a divine purpose could have been allowed to
depend so largely on forgeries for its substructure
at critical epochs, as the Roman system has in fact
depended."

Whether this autocracy works well or ill is
another question. It certainly makes for smooth-
ness and a surface efficiency. Orders are obeyed.
Rough edges can be rounded off without the
trouble and delay which so often occur while
committees, or elected bodies, are reasoned with,

and their consents secured. If one may judge by the analogy of the political world the nations of Europe are to-day preferring the efficiency of autocracy to liberty. But it must be remembered that these absolutist nations make power their first and principal aim. If the first aim of a nation is to have the most efficient and powerful armed forces possible there is much to be said for absolutism in some shape as most likely to attain this end.

But, obviously, even if, which God forbid, this were to be the generally recognized ideal of nations as political entities, the Church must aim at something quite different. Its first aim must be to bear witness to Christ. Absolutism is clean contrary to the spirit of Christ and His Apostles. Freedom provides the only climate in which the Christian spirit can thrive. Even if religious autocracy could be shown to produce better results than are produced under any other system the price paid, namely, the strangulation of freedom, would be too high.

But it is at least open to doubt whether in the moral and spiritual sphere the absolutist system is in the end more efficient than one based on freedom. The career of the great John Henry Newman, perhaps the greatest religious genius

of the century, for the thirty years after his seces-
sion in 1845, is the story of hope deferred, frus-
tration, and waste. It has been the same with the
treatment of the modernist. Without freedom
the mind languishes, difficulties are driven under-
ground, and truth suffers. When in the seventies and eighties of the last century new theories of
evolution and new critical knowledge together
made current theories of inspiration untenable for
scholars, the freedom of the Church of England
enabled Charles Gore and his friends to show that
no one need discard the Catholic faith on account
of holding these new theories. The Roman
autocracy treated the modernist very differently.
" Venerable brethren," wrote Pius X in 1907 in
his encyclical *Pascendi Gregis* to the Bishops of the
Roman Church, " it will be your first duty to
resist such victims of pride, to employ them in the
lowest and obscurest offices."

The whole atmosphere of the New Testament
is one of freedom. " I do not see how any honest
inquirer," wrote Dr. C. H. Turner, " can read and
judge the New Testament as a whole without
being conscious that an atmosphere of freedom
was one of the essential constituents of the life of
the Apostolic Church ; not the only constituent,
of course, but a constituent and an essential one.

The freedom was not merely a negative freedom from the shackles of the land : it was something positive. Each member of the body has his part and function, without which the other members fail of their completeness : and if he must not work out his part in isolation from the rest, neither must they impose on him such limitation as to deprive him of all initiative. But this mark of the Christian fellowship, as the New Testament represents it, the Roman Church has to all appearance lost. We may well believe that the famous boast of Cardinal Bonnechose, ' I say to my clergy, " March " and they march,' would be translated into less autocratic language to-day. Yet the subordination of laity to the clergy, clergy to Bishops, Bishops to Pope even if interpreted more liberally than by the French prelate, can hardly by any stretch of charity be brought into harmonious relation, with the ideal drawn from us in the Apostolic Age."[1]

If we turn to the non-episcopal Churches we find that they reject firmly the idea that any one kind of authority is essential, claiming the right to choose their own form of government. " It (the Welsh Presbyterian Church) does not believe that any one particular form of ministry is divinely

[1] C. H. Turner, *Catholic and Apostolic*, p. 104.

instituted, and is for that reason immutable. Rather we are of opinion that the history of the Church proves that under the guidance of the Spirit different arrangements were entrusted to the wisdom of the Church, as we see in the Episcopal, Presbyterian and Congregational Churches, and moreover believe that we shall again trust to the wisdom and spiritual sense of the United Church to order its ministry."[1] This extract from the response of the Presbyterian Church of Wales to the Report of the Conference on Faith and Order held at Lausanne in 1927 not unfairly sums up the general attitude of the non-episcopal Churches to the ministry, and indirectly to the *magisterium* of the Church.

The *Via Media* while rejecting autocracy has retained Bishops as an essential part of its constitution.

The Bishop according to ancient tradition is the leader and constitutional ruler in his Diocese, besides being the appointed channel for the transmission of holy orders. The word *constitutional* is important because the idea sometimes gets abroad that the Bishop is an autocrat. " With

---

[1] *Convictions*. A Selection from the Responses of the Churches to the Report of the World Conference on Faith and Order held at Lausanne in 1927, p. 93. (Edited by Leonard Hodgson.)

us," once wrote J. H. Newman to a Roman Catholic friend, " every Bishop is a Pope in his own diocese." This he should not be, though he was something very like it in Newman's time. An autocrat is a begetter of autocracies. Under the autocracy of the Pope every Bishop tends to become an autocrat, subject only to the Pope, witness Newman's own experiences, but it was not so in the early Church. The position of the Greek king in Homer furnishes a close analogy to that of the Bishop in the primitive Church. The Homeric king, like the Highland chief, was the chief executive officer and the presiding judge. He was the fount of authority and the spring of action, and occupied a quasi-paternal position with regard to his subjects. But though there was something sacred about his authority he was no autocrat. He had a Council of Elders, who advised, while the more important matters, such as questions of peace or war, were submitted to a popular assembly.

In the same way the primitive Bishop was supposed to consult his Presbyters—it must be remembered that dioceses were very small—and, though the kind of questions on which a popular vote was necessary did not arise, on the very important occasion of the election of a new Bishop the name of the man chosen by the elders was submitted for approval to the whole Church in the diocese concerned.

The Churches of the *Via Media* have, whatever their differences, given both clergy and laity a share in the government of the Church. This is true even of the Church of England, though partly owing to its State connexion the Church of England stands in a class apart. For any canon passed in the Upper House of the Convocations of Canterbury or York requires among other things the concurrence of the Lower House of the Province before it becomes effective. This control however is provincial, not diocesan. Besides the rights of the clergy exercised in their Convocations the laity have a good deal of power on matters not immediately concerned with doctrine. In practice no law directly affecting the Church is considered by Parliament unless it has previously been passed by a majority of the Bishops, Clergy and Laity, in the Church Assembly. As it is open to any twelve members of the Assembly to demand a vote by houses, this proceeding gives to any one house a power of veto over new legislation. Apart from the Church Assembly there is in each diocese a Diocesan Conference consisting of clergy and laity, over which the

Bishop presides. It exercises no authority over worship or doctrine. It can only offer advice, or criticism, with the Bishop's permission, but it controls finance, and so exercises real power, though not so much as might appear, as a Diocesan Conference is unlikely to oppose the expressed wishes of the Bishop, though it may criticize them.

The same principle of giving both clergy and laity a real share in both provincial and diocesan government prevails throughout the Anglican Communion, though elsewhere than in England it is less hampered by the tie with the State.

We may contrast with the position of the laity in the *Via Media* Monsignor Talbot's famous letter to Cardinal Manning when the Roman Catholic laity had presented an address of confidence to John Henry Newman in 1867; "the most offensive production," wrote Talbot, "that has appeared in England since the time of Dr. Milner, and if a check be not placed on the laity of England they will be the rulers of the Catholic Church instead of the Holy See and the Episcopate." "What is the Province of the laity?" he asked indignantly. "To hunt, to shoot, to entertain? These matters they understand, but to meddle with ecclesiastical matters they have no right at all."[1]

As in the Eastern Church it is natural for Anglicanism to organize itself nationally. The Church in each nation forms itself into what in the East would be an independent patriarchate and has no formal connexion with any other. For instance, since its Disestablishment the Welsh Church has held its own Synods and Conferences independently of the Church of England. Each makes its own canons and acts for itself. Inter-communion, of course, exists and unity of faith is preserved by loyalty to the creeds, while though each has its own prayer-book they all adhere in essentials to the Book of Common Prayer. By no means all have retained the Thirty-nine Articles.

Organic unity is preserved by a common adherence to the historic episcopate and insistence on the transmission of holy orders through the Bishop.

[1] *Life of Cardinal Manning*, Purcell, II, 317.

CHAPTER VI

MAGISTERIAL AUTHORITY IN THE CHURCH OF ENGLAND

" I mentioned to him how common it was in the world to tell absurd stories of him, and to ascribe to him very strange sayings. Johnson, ' What do they make me say, sir ? ' Boswell, ' Why, sir, as an instance very strange indeed (laughing heartily as I spoke), David Hume told me you said you would stand before a battery of cannon to restore Convocation to its full powers.' Little did I apprehend that he had actually said this : but I was soon convinced of my error ; for, with a determined look he thundered out, ' And would I not, sir ? Shall the Presbyterian Kirk of Scotland have its General Assembly, and the Church of England be denied its Convocation ? ' He was walking up and down the room while I told him the anecdote ; but when he uttered this explosion of high-church zeal he had come close to my chair, and his eyes flashed with indignation." Boswell's *Life of Samuel Johnson.*

" In England there are the Free Churches whose ministry has in recent years been enormously influenced, if vaguely, in the Catholic direction, but which will not readily submit to the undemocratic system of Rome with its various evil consequences, or to the Erastianism of the Anglican Church."

Newman Smyth, *Passing Protestantism and
Coming Catholicism.*

NOW in respect to this magisterial authority the Church of England is in a class by itself. There are people who say " There is no magisterial authority in the Church of England." Nor would such a taunt be altogether without foundation. There is, indeed, far more authority exercised than critics give the Church credit for. But though it may be true that only the exceptional cases get into the press, nevertheless there is a residuum of defiance of all magisterial authority which has no parallel in any other religious body in Christendom. Devoted priests from time to time announce their intention of defying their Bishops while their flocks applaud. " Many priests—and I for one "—recently wrote a Parish Priest to the *Church Times*,[1] " will decline to consult either bishops or chancellors about Reservation or aumbries. We shall reserve without even a reference of grace to the Bishop, and we shall feel compelled to put either an aumbry, tabernacle or hanging-pyx, without a faculty in our churches." There is not a word in his letter to show that in thus defying his Bishop and all *magisterium* in the Church of England he is doing anything out of the way. When the late Lord Davidson became

[1] July 24, 1936.

Archbishop of Canterbury in 1903, he had been successively Chaplain to Archbishop Tait, Dean of Windsor, Bishop of Rochester, and Bishop of Winchester. No one in the Church of England knew its state better from the point of view of those who have to govern, and his first important action was to induce the government to appoint a Commission on Ecclesiastical Discipline. The name is significant. The Commission reported in 1906. " Clergymen," it stated, " have claimed the liberty, and even asserted the duty, of disobedience to the decisions of a tribunal, the authority of which they repudiate." " The machinery of discipline," it went on to assert, " has broken down." The thirty years which have elapsed since that Report was published have seen no improvement.

Now this light-hearted spirit of defiance is in marked contrast to the Anglo-Catholic attitude a hundred years ago. " The lightest word of a Bishop spoken *ex cathedra*," wrote Newman in 1837, "is law." When in 1837 the Bishop of Oxford made some animadversions on the Tracts, Newman offered to suppress them altogether, an offer which John Keble approved. In 1851 Samuel Wilberforce expressed a wish, without issuing a formal inhibition that Pusey would not officiate in the

Diocese of Oxford, Pusey protested but submitted.[1]

In the next generation Mr. Bennett of St. Paul's, Knightsbridge, resigned when he found himself unable to submit to the demands of Bishop Blomfield. Mr. Bryan King of St. George's-in-the-East in 1859 gave up the eucharistic vestments at the request of Bishop Tait. Those who refused to obey did so with extreme reluctance and only because in disobeying their Bishop they felt they were obeying the Prayer Book, which bound them both. This attitude is the more remarkable when we consider the notoriously partisan character of the episcopal appointments. From the time that the Tractarians began to attract general attention, until Mr. Gladstone became Prime Minister in 1869 with the exception of Walter Ker Hamilton, Bishop of Salisbury 1854–1869, no High Churchman was made a Bishop, while many who became Bishops were open and avowed opponents of Tractarianism and all its works.

[1] Samuel Wilberforce who became Bishop of Oxford in 1845 never was a High Churchman, but the mere suspicion of it, owing to his sympathetic treatment of the religious houses in the diocese of Oxford, kept him from higher office until 1869, when he became Bishop of Winchester.

There has been, therefore, a complete change of mind and disposition.

If we seek to find the cause of the present lack of discipline it is tempting to find it in the connexion of the Church in England with the State. The English Church alone of all the Churches of the *Via Media* has this trouble. The English Church alone is established. Therefore the State connexion is the *fons et origo* of the trouble. But the Irish Church was not disestablished until 1869 and the Welsh Church not till 1919, yet both these Churches were law-abiding and peaceful before the connexion with the State was dissolved. Moreover, as we have seen in the English Church great deference to authority was shown until the seventies of the last century. The reason for the change, then, cannot be the State connexion; it will, however, be found in the history of the Church.

In considering its history we must remember that the trouble has been mainly over ceremonial and that the chief bone of contention has been the so-called Ornaments Rubric which runs:

The Morning and Evening Prayer shall be used in the accustomed Place of the Church, Chapel or Chancel except it shall be otherwise determined by the Ordinary of the Place. And the Chancels shall remain as they have done in times past.

And here is to be noted, that such Ornaments of the Church, and of the Ministers thereof, at all Times of their Ministration, shall be retained, and be in use, as were in this Church of England, by the Authority of Parliament, in the Second Year of the Reign of King Edward the Sixth.

The second year of King Edward the Sixth is generally agreed to be the year of the publication of the First Prayer Book of that reign, which was published in January 154⅞.

At first the failure to obey the ceremonial directions of the Prayer Book lay in defect, not excess. Matthew Parker and John Whitgift, Elizabeth's first and third Archbishops strove with indifferent success to secure as a minimum that the priest should wear a surplice while officiating, and that he should practise a ceremonial which included, at the least, administering to communicants who were kneeling, and using the sign of the cross in baptism. Later on William Laud laboured indefatigably in the same direction and with greater success. It is to be noted that Nonconformists, as they were called, that is those who refused to conform to the ceremonial requirements of the Prayer Book, were treated with leniency. Even Laud deprived very few on account of ceremonial irregularity. It was the Separatists who refused to come to

Church at all and set up separate conventicles who experienced harsh treatment. The more determined Nonconformists, however, abandoned the Church after the Savoy Conference in 1662, and, as far as discipline went, there was no trouble for nearly 200 years. But for the greater part of that period it was the peace of death, not the controlled activity of ordered life. There was no trouble because no Bishop attempted to enforce the requirements of the Prayer Book. There was a very common neglect of duty and little or no attempt to correct what was amiss.

When the revival began in 1833 there was naturally tension between those who desired to arouse the sleepers and restore forgotten doctrine and practices, and those who either did not wish to be roused, or at any rate to be roused in that particular way. The trouble became widespread when the movement spread to the parishes and expressed itself in services, vestments, and ceremonial. When complaints were made to the Bishops most of them not unnaturally took the line of scolding the innovators for reviving, as they put it, obsolete rubrics, and there ensued a period of strained relations between the inno- vating clergy desirous of reviving practices enjoined by the Prayer Book, even at the cost of

N

stirring up strife, and the Bishops who wished to preserve peace even if rubrics continued to be disobeyed. This state of things went on for more than twenty years. It was generally taken for granted that the offending clergymen had the law on their side. Most of those whose conduct was called in question obeyed their Bishop under protest. Few were recalcitrant. Those who were could plead that they refused to obey the *magisterium* of the Bishop because they were obeying the higher authority of the Prayer Book, which bound both alike.

If matters could have been left in this state they would have righted themselves. Bishops would have applied the brake and on the other hand they, and church-people generally, would have learned that there was more to be said for practices they disliked than they realized. The novelty would have worn off. English people have a strong sense of justice, though they may be obstinate and slow to see the force of new opinions ; no set of men would have been harshly treated indefinitely, whose only crime was excess of zeal in obeying the law. But whatever prospect there was of arriving at a reasonable *modus vivendi* in this way was shattered by two legal decisions and an Act of Parliament.

In two famous cases, the Purchas case (1871) and Clifton *v*. Ridsdale (1877), the Judicial Committee of the Privy Council, to all intents and purposes, inserted a *not* into the Ornaments Rubric, and for the next twenty-five years the Bishops instead of restraining the advanced clergy from being too zealous in obeying the law, were urging upon them the strictest obedience to it. " We," wrote the Bishops in a joint pastoral issued on March 1, 1875, " the clergy, are bound by every consideration to obey when called upon by lawful authority ; to disobey is to set an example that cannot fail to be most injurious in its effects."

Unfortunately the word *lawful* was a question-begging epithet. Anglo-Catholics firmly refused to accept the lawfulness of the authority. They believed that the judgements were judgements of policy, or in the words of John Taylor Coleridge, who had himself been a judge for twenty-three years, " it " (the judgement in the Purchas case) " repealed the law it professed to interpret." The *Church Times* spoke " of the notorious fact that the decision of the Court (in the Ridsdale case) is openly branded by an eminent member of it as ' a miscarriage of justice '." It is not necessary to argue whether this view of the judgement was justified or not. The point is that the High Church party believed it was, and that belief changed their attitude to authority.

Holding the view they did the clergy might have taken the line that the decision was plainly unjust, and therefore need not be obeyed, quoting Hampden and his refusal to pay Ship-Money. Instead they declared that the Judicial Committee of the Privy Council was a secular court and, as such, had no jurisdiction in an ecclesiastical case. Here again whether they were right or wrong is not the question. The point is that they thought they were. In consequence they looked on disobedience to the law, and to the Bishop, so far as he was helping to administer the law, as a sacred duty.

The situation was very much aggravated by the Public Worship Regulation Act (1874), drawn up by Archbishop Tait, egged on by Queen Victoria and Lord Shaftesbury, which was introduced as a Bill "to put down Ritualism." The Act had no authority from Convocation, and while it fanned the flame of disobedience, its coercive measures resulted in five priests going to prison. The spectacle of hard-working clergymen being sent to jail because they refused to obey the judgement of a Court it was against their conscience to acknowledge, caused so much scandal that prosecutions ceased and the Act became a dead letter.

The trial of the Bishop of Lincoln before the Archbishop of Canterbury was the last great ritual trial. Since then the Bishops have been left to deal with their clergy as best they can without help from the coercive power of the law. In other words, they are left to cope with a difficult situation armed with their own spiritual authority and the rules of a Prayer Book, which is in part obsolete.

Unfortunately a tradition of defiance of episcopal and legal authority has been handed down. The Anglo-Catholic heroes, not to mention those who went to prison, men like Charles Lowder, A. H. Mackonochie, Arthur Stanton, Robert Dolling, were all men who were at one time or another defying the law, and in some cases their Bishop as well. These men are widely revered, and the injustice from which they are thought to have suffered has bred a widespread contempt for law as applied to the Church, and has weakened incalculably episcopal authority. We have, indeed, travelled a long way from the Tractarians.

There is one not unimportant difference between the recalcitrants yesterday and those of fifty years ago. Those who disobeyed their Bishops and Privy Council judgements in the last century claimed in all good faith to be obeying the directions of the Prayer Book. Since then the researches of Dr. Wickham Legg, Mr. Cuthbert Atchley, Mr. F. C. Eeles and others have shown that the authority for some of the things they introduced was not the Prayer Book but Rome, and modern Rome at that. The recalcitrants of that day disobeyed through ignorance both as to " how the Chancels stood in time past " and what the Ornaments of the Minister actually were in the second year of King Edward the Sixth, taking for granted that the vestments and practices they saw on the Continent were those contemplated by the Book of Common Prayer. The recalcitrants of to-day have shifted their ground and finding it difficult to justify themselves on the ground of strict obedience to the Prayer Book, plead somewhat vaguely the authority, or tradition, of " the Western Church," denying by implication the authority of the thirty-fourth article, which affirms that : " Every particular or national Church hath authority to ordain, change and abolish, ceremonies and rites of the Church ordained only of man's authority, so that all things be done to edifying," as well as rejecting that palladium of the persecuted ritualist, the Ornaments Rubric.

The force of this appeal to " the Western Church " is undermined by the fact that the Church of England has asserted its independence in greater matters.   It has allowed the clergy to marry ; it allows criticism of the Bible which is contrary to the express commands of Rome ; it stands by an ordinal which Rome declares to be so defective as to make our ordinations invalid. Most important of all it refuses to acknowledge the Supremacy of the Pope which is the keystone of the Roman arch. Father Woodlock has told us that belief in papal infallibility is as much an article of the Roman faith as belief in the Incarnation. It seems an irrational exercise of private judgement to pick and choose as to the matters in which we accept the *magisterium* of Rome and in which we flout it.   To quote Bishop Gore : [1]

" Romanism without the practical recognition of the Pope is an extraordinarily irrational and inconsequential system of ideas. I am quite sure that an Anglican Churchman who wants his beliefs to be rational must not think that he can borrow the system of Roman belief or practice, either leaving out in theory or ignoring in fact

[1] *The Basis of Anglican Fellowship*, p. 46.

the authority of the Pope. To accept the Anglican position as valid, in any sense, is to appeal behind the Pope and the authority of the mediæval Church which developed the papacy, to the undivided Church, and with the undivided Church to Scripture, as limiting for ever the articles of faith to the original creed."

The Future.

It is when we come to consider remedies we see that the State connexion is a hindrance. It holds up reform. Legislation is almost impossible if the subject of legislation rouses strong feeling and without legislation there is no possibility of revising the Prayer Book or creating a Court of Final Appeal which will command respect. Further, though this point is debatable, it seems reasonable to suppose that the Bishops would have an additional claim to the obedience of their clergy, if the clergy had had some voice in their appointment, or, at the least, reasonable security against the appointment of men chosen by the State to grind some particular national, or party, axe. The motives which guided sovereigns and statesmen in making political appointments before 1870 may seem to belong to a state of things which has passed away never to return. Yet we have not to look very far to see how swiftly moral standards can deteriorate : and we are bound therefore to admit the possibility that most unsuitable appointments may be made under the existing system against which the Church would, as things are, have no power to protect itself. Since the discipline of the clergy depends on the moral and spiritual authority of the Bishops it seems not unimportant that those over whom authority is to be exercised should be able to regard the choice of the Bishop who is to rule over them as unaffected by even the suspicion of some unworthy motive.

Let me conclude this chapter with two final observations. Though it is true that this want of magisterial authority exists and is a definite weakness of the Church of England, it can easily be exaggerated. The number of recalcitrant clergy as compared with the whole is very small. The clergy of the Church of England as a whole are as law-abiding and dutiful as any other. The rebels are few and are conspicuous out of all proportion to their numbers. Secondly, whatever we may think of the Church of England we must remember that the weaknesses in government are peculiar to it ; they are not characteristic of the *Via Media*. They are the accidents incidental to its history, and are not of its essence. The Commission on Church and State, which has just reported, has made recommendations with a view to remedying these weaknesses. Some will think that their proposals go too far to have any chance of securing the consent of Parliament. Others will reject them off-hand as not going far enough to secure reasonable liberty for the Church. But it is enough here to say that they show that after its long slumber the giant is waking up : he has partly opened his eyes and is trying to stretch his limbs and sooner or later will burst his bonds. In the memorable words of Archbishop Davidson, "it is a fundamental principle that the Church, that is the Bishops, together with the Clergy and Laity, must in the last resort, when its mind has been fully ascertained, retain its inalienable right, in loyalty to our Lord and Saviour Jesus Christ, to formulate its faith in Him, and to arrange the expression of that Holy Faith in its form of Worship."[1]

[1] Adopted in a resolution passed by the Church Assembly, February 5, 1930.

CHAPTER VII

THE GENIUS OF THE VIA MEDIA

" Episcopacy holds the key to the door through which other churches may be invited to enter into a catholicism large enough to hold them all."

" The Episcopal Church by virtue of its tradition and position has, as no other, I am venturing to say, the opportunity and the call to become the mediating Church among all the Churches."

NEWMAN SMYTH, *Passing Protestantism and Coming Catholicism.*

WE sometimes speak of the genius of a people, meaning something intangible, and indefinable, but a permanent reality which we can comprehend, that manifests itself in all that people's most characteristic sayings and doings, in its history and its literature. The genius of the *Via Media* as we have seen lies in an obstinate adherence to principles which are apparently inconsistent with one another, which it holds in a working synthesis without pushing any one of them to its presumably logical conclusion, or attempting to define their respective powers with precision. It is faithful on the one hand to the *given* element in religion, treating scripture and tradition as co-ordinate authorities, though sub-ordinating tradition to scripture in one very important respect, when it makes scriptural authority necessary for any belief, which is to be held as necessary to salvation. On the other it admits the full force of those monitors within the soul, which we call reason and intuition, under-standing of course that intuition may be divinely inspired.

The *Via Media* therefore imposes no strait jacket. It appeals to reasonable men and women. It asks no one to believe as a matter of faith any doctrine which his mind rejects as unreasonable any more than it requires him to accept as religious truth anything which his conscience assures him to be wrong. He is neither required to believe that there are no errors in Holy Scripture, nor that it was ever right for the Church to burn people alive in this world or that a merciful God would burn people for ever and ever in the next.

" The Roman Catholic found infallibility in the visible Church ; the Puritan delighted in literal obedience to the word of Scripture ; the Quaker listened to the voice of God speaking in his conscience ; and the rationalist found the truth in his intellectual apprehension of it. This is not to say that no Quaker read his Bible, or that no Roman Catholic used his reason. But the ultimate court of appeal for each lay in the direction which he had elected to follow and the conclusion thence received was cogent and for him unanswerable. The High Church Anglican clung to his four-fold strand of belief and made up for want of logic by the undoubted advantage of not being dependent on a single means of support."[1] If I may substitute " the follower of the *Via Media*" for "the High Church Anglican," I think this gives a rough summary of the position.

In the sphere of government the *Via Media* also endeavours to embrace at once the principle of authority transmitted down the ages, tracing its descent to the Apostles, and at the same time the principle of freedom, allowing both the presbyters and faithful laity a constitutional place in the Church's government.

The Church of England has been often called a Bridge Church, and as such symbolizes and gathers up in itself one of the main functions of the *Via Media* because in her as the potential link between two opposite banks lies the main hope of future reunion. It would, I believe, be the greatest disaster to the cause of ultimate reunion should we through impatience, or out of a

[1] Clarke, *Short History of the Christian Church.*

mistaken sense of generosity, or from good-nature, or fear of being thought narrow-minded, or through intolerance of our own short-comings, let one end of the bridge fall into the stream so that it ceased to be a bridge.

Such a break down was threatened in 1934 when a Unitarian was allowed to preach in an English Cathedral, but the action of the Bishop who gave permission for the sermon was promptly disowned by the other Bishops of the Province, and the incident served to show up the loyalty of the English Church to the historic faith. But for this disavowal it might have seemed, to quote the Bishop of Durham, "that the vital truth of Christ's Deity was so lightly esteemed by the Church of England that even its explicit denial was not disregarded as a disqualification for admission to her pulpits." The Bridge would certainly break if in any scheme of reunion we ceased to stipulate that the Historic Episcopate and an episcopally ordained ministry should be retained in any United Church of the future. Here let me quote from a very weighty pronouncement by the Archbishop of Canterbury to his Diocesan Conference.[1]

" There is another consideration which we

[1] From the *Church Times*, July 15, 1934.

must keep before our minds. Many outside our own communion have shared the hope that the Anglican Church by virtue of its distinctive character and witness might prove to be what has been called a Bridge Church. At one end it has affinity with the great Latin Church of the West and with the Orthodox Churches of the East : and at the other with the various Protestant Churches. It is natural that some of our members should stress one affinity rather than another. But it would be disastrous if this double stress were to imperil the unity of our fellowship. A bridge is useless which consists merely of ends and breaks in the middle. There is real danger lest in seeking union with our Christian brethren, at one end or the other, we should impair our own. Rather we must address ourselves to the task of strengthening our own unity, of bringing together the elements which in history and in fact co-exist in our own Church life, not merely by a somewhat impatient tolerance, but in the reality of a fellowship, in which each is welcomed as contributing to the life of the whole body."

The *Via Media* is something far bigger than the Church of England or even of Anglicanism. Nor do I look forward to a reunited Church of the future which is merely a glorified Church of

England. Nevertheless, under the providence of God the Church of England rediscovered and, in course of time, propagated, certain principles vital in the life of the Church, that were in danger of being forgotten. We do both ourselves, and other religious communions, and the sacred cause of charity itself, a real disservice if we belittle our own achievement. "Hold fast that which thou hast that no man take thy crown."

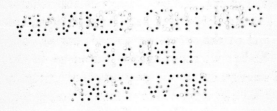

Printed in Great Britain by the KEMP HALL PRESS, LTD.
in the City of Oxford